Legacy of an African Freedom Fighter

By Bol Gai Deng

As told to

Andrea P. McDaniel/American Epiphany™

September 2018

For information: *www.kushdemocraticmajority.org,*
www.americanepiphany.org.

Email: *bolgaideng@gmail.com*
apmcdaniel25@yahoo.com

FIRST EDITION

Cover images by Don Blake

Graphics by James Manship

ISBN 978-1-7326284-0-3
ISBN 978-1-7326284-1-0 (ebook)

"I dreamt many times that all the young men in our generation will get worse and worse until one day a boy... from Aweil will come over from the US and take over. Then gradually Sudan will develop into a nation of peace, justice and from God."

~~Njalueth Makor
Kush Democratic Majority Party
Australia

In Memory of my Grandfather, Deng Kuol Gai,

and dedicated to the people

of South Sudan and Sudan

CONTENTS

FOREWORD

I became aware of the horrors perpetrated on the African people of Sudan by those claiming to be Arabs while I was gaining consciousness of the struggles of John Garang against the Khartoum regime. This helped me to understand the immense problem of Arab racism that was rampant in Sudan and other parts of countries in the north of Africa. Bol Gai Deng hails from South Sudan, a land where the Nile River lingers, gathering traditions and history before making its way north.

The story being told by Bol Gai Deng is not extraordinary; it is real and it is still relevant. What is extraordinary is that this young man has overcome all of the obstacles placed in his path to pronounce the truth about what was happening in his country. This fact is known by all of those who specialize in contemporary African history and culture.

What the government of President Bashir has specialized in doing is to *confuse* the American and European publics. They have been master propagandists and this is the reason the continuing Darfur crisis is no longer front and center in the minds of African Americans or other Americans. However, the crisis in Sudan is a persistent one that will not disappear until Arab racism disappears.

It was easy for African Americans to fight against the South African regime because it was a familiar case of white or European racism against African people. However, in the case of Sudan the lines seem blurred only because we cannot discern the extent of the Arab hatred of Africans whose land they have expropriated like the Europeans had done in Southern Africa. Both groups assumed the inferiority of African people and felt that they had to attack Africans in order to gain control over the vast territories of wealth owned by Africans.

The mistake for the African American is based on two false conclusions. The first is that they believe the Khartoum Arab regime identifies with the historic movement of African people. This conclusion is one based on the fact that the Arabs often have the same complexion as the Africans that they do not identify with as brothers or sisters. The Arabs have forgotten their grandparents' African languages if they ever knew them and have declared themselves to be "different" from the inheritors of the land.

Rarely does an Arab in Sudan identify with the legitimate struggles of the Africans for liberation, equality, and control over their own destiny. It would almost be unthinkable for the Arab minority of fifteen percent who control the Sudanese government. So the first conclusion is that the color of the Arabs is the same as ours and therefore they must be for the same objectives as other Pan African people. This was a horrible conclusion often made by President Obama, Susan Rice and Congresswoman Bass who was designated by the Congressional Black Caucus as the one who should speak on this issue. They are beguiled by color and looks and not by the historical realities of the Arab consciousness and culture that seek to dominate African people in Sudan and elsewhere in the north of the continent.

The second conclusion is that the struggle in Sudan is one of religion. Of course, many Americans see the situation as one of religion. However, the Darfurians and many other black Sudanese are Muslims; yet their religion does not keep them from being attacked by the Arab government in Khartoum. I think that African Americans are also confused because of the Nation of Islam and other Islamic groups in our communities. They have confused Arabism and Islam and in their protection of their religious liberties have defended the worst elements of Arab racism. Unfortunately, what I have observed, as well as Brother Bankie Bankie, is the fact that African Americans are so confused by Islam that they want to attack the African Sudanese in the name of Islam just as the Arabs are doing right now.

I call upon all freedom loving and mature Africans to take a stand against the regime that is assaulting our people in that country. The Africans are suffering every day. Their homes are bombed and their children are maimed and they are enslaved, even today, in the homes of rich Arab people. This is far worse than the situation was in South Africa.

The SPLA, Sudanese People Liberation Army, fought in the south to liberate their territory and were successful in 2011. Yet the conspiracy to steal the resources of South Sudan was already in place when the new government sat in Juba. There was confusion because neither Salva Kiir nor Riek Machar, President and Vice President, were statesmen. They had neither the knowledge nor the vision of the late John Garang who had been steeped in Afrocentric Pan Africanism and had exchanged notes with the great philosopher Kwasi Prah in Juba.

So the South Sudan situation must be worked out and the largest ethnic groups, the Dinka and the Nuer, must not be manipulated by outside forces that will allow the emergence of the Arab racists in South Sudan as another component of the humiliation of the African people. We must fight every instance to change the historiography of northern Africa and that is the reason we must protect the Kushite and Nubian heritages of Sudan from the distortion of Arab Islamic historians.

The archaeology of a new praxis must be grounded in the realization that education, all knowledge production is a *political act*. The nature of the politics is to gain control over the narrative of land, relationships, and visions of the future. Our intellectuals have warned of the Afro-Arab Borderlands conflict as the problem of the 21st century for Africa. It will not just be a struggle over Blue Nile,

Abyei, Southern Kordofan, Darfur, and South Sudan; the struggle will find its way to Mali, it already has, and to Niger, Cameroon, Central African Republic, and other countries. The African Nation must have a sense of itself and must assert its identity within the context of a national constituency.

Writing the foreword to this book by a passionate and brilliant young Sudanese, Bol Gai Deng, is a profound honor because he knows that the other apartheids are in Sudan and Mauritania. Fighting against them must be our constant battle or else we are to soon see the end of any assertion of African culture. Bankie is right to see the struggle in Sudan, and in South Sudan, as one that can be called the "cockpit of Africa." None of us can have ignorance any longer, none of us can say that we do not know what is happening to Africans on their own continent; the entire continent of Africa and its diaspora must rise up once against to confront racist antagonism by invaders and intruders who seek to enforce their dictates on an ancient people.

North Africa was completely populated by black people, long before the coming of the Arabs, and the Arabs not the Europeans conducted the first forced migration of Africans out of Africa. Bol Gai Deng was enslaved by the Arabs but emerged as you will see from this very powerful book to become a conscious Pan African.

Dr. Molefi Kete Asante, Chair, Department of African American Studies
Temple University
Editor-in-Chief: *Journal of Black Studies*

INTRODUCTION

The event that changed my happy childhood forever occurred in 1987 when my older brother Makuach Gai Deng, his wife and I were kidnapped from our Aweil village in South Sudan by the Mujahideen or Janjaweed (Arabic for "armed horsemen") and sold to Arab slavemasters. Out of the seven hundred children abducted and forced on the 200-plus-mile march to Dhein (also known as Ed Da'ein), many were lost.

At our last rest stop, the Arab slavers decided to teach us a lesson. We were forced to watch as they cut off the heads of several children using a *"saif,"* Arabic for a "big, long knife," which in English means *"sword."**

This horrific 'lesson' was forever seared into my soul. I was seven years old and petrified to see such powerful men butcher young children. The terrorists wanted us to walk faster and not try to escape. Those of us who survived struggled in terror to keep up, knowing that we would not see our families again.

One young girl could not stop her tears. She finally said she couldn't walk any longer. For that she was beaten and for three days forced to carry the bloody, decapitated head of another child. It was a brutal warning meant for all of us that if we tried to escape, slow down, or cried, we would be next. This brave, young girl told the Arab slave traders that cutting off someone's head is against Muoyjang, or Dinka, culture. A dead person must be honored and receive a burial. She asked one of the Arab Sudanese slave catchers,

---

The Arabs carried "saifs" with them as second weapons along with AK 47 rifles. Dr. A. Rahman Zaky writes about the saif as an "Arab sword, found in most countries where the Arabs have lived."[1] The sword is also found on the flag of Saudi Arabia's King. Mecca, Saudi Arabia is the birthplace of Muhammad and considered the holiest site in Islam.[2]

"Yengolui yin hen ke cit ekene?" Dinka for "Please, why are you doing this to me?" Her pleas were ignored.

Those of us who managed to survive to the city of Dhein*, the last stop, were separated into groups and sold to work as domestic and farm slaves to Arabs plantation owners. The women were valuable as sex slaves who could bear children and increase the Arab population.

The horrible nightmares we lived through are with me every day and will be for the rest of my life. I pray continually to God that I never forget my family's legacy of *"Nhialic Madhol"* which is Dinka for "the energy to help the suffering people of Sudan" because they do not deserve to go through these horrors. These murdered children were innocents, but because they were African blacks, Arabs considered them worthless and should be snuffed out for crying or walking too slowly.

---

*Dhein or Ed Da'ein in western Sudan not only saw Bol and others sold into slavery but on March 27-28, 1987 more than a thousand other Dinka men, women and children were killed, many burned to death by Rizeigat Arabs and others in the town. An investigation of the slavery and massacre can be found in "Slavery in the Sudan: Human Rights Abuses in Sudan 1987" by Ushari Ahmad Mahmud and Suleyman Ali Baldo, July 1987.

PROLOGUE: MY GRANDFATHER'S LEGACY

In 1881, an Arab Sudanese Islamic cleric named Muhammad Ahmad, who subscribed to an apocalyptic strain of Islam, had just proclaimed himself Mahdi which means "guided one" and was determined to restore the glory of Islam throughout the entire world.*

His troops began a political and military Islamic revolution against the Egyptian government which had controlled Sudan since 1820. Sudanese African males had been forced into the Egyptian military and other members of the local African population were sold into slavery. The Egyptian provincial governor also took absolute control of Sudanese trade which further destroyed African Sudanese livelihoods and culture.

A new Egyptian governor in 1863 initiated an anti-slave campaign (and was joined by the British in 1874). His campaign was vehemently opposed by *Arab* Sudanese who had built the slave trade into a critical part of their economy. The indigent *African* population was caught in the middle but then as now, refused to buckle under Arab domination of their land.

My Grandfather, Deng Kuol Gai, was well known for his heroism against the Arab soldiers. His brother Mayen Deng Gai was captured and believed enslaved and/or killed by Al Mahdi's troops soon after the Islamic revolution began. My grandfather did not hesitate and prepared for battle. Grandfather led the Dinka tribe to push the Arab slave traders out of the Aweil Region known as Bour Raal in the Korok area.

The Arab Islamic invaders were heavily armed with rifles and

The 1881 Islamic Revolution is further explored in Chapter 2.

long knives. Deng met with his Chief and outlined a plan to defend against the Al Mahdi's aggressive attacks. The plan was very risky for the entire tribe. In the end, the Chief agreed to a ruse to turn over to the enemy the tribe's most precious assets, their women and their cows. Their women were irreplaceable and the cows symbolized their wealth.

The plan put the women in the front of the turnover party followed by hundreds of cows. Unbeknownst to the invaders, Dinka fighters hid between the cows with Grandfather Deng Kuol Gai at the very front. Though Al-Mahdi's Generals Zubair Pasha and Hussein Ben Merriam (who was more widely known as Abu Merriam) were surrounded by gun-toting guards, Deng, armed with only a spear, charged the heavily guarded Commander Meriam. Meriam's guards opened fire and my grandfather was shot three times but he did not stop. Deng and his spear went right through the crowd, landing a direct hit on Meriam that proved fatal. The guards' bullets, even at point blank range, miraculously did not pierce my grandfather's body. Family historians say he was protected because he was a spiritual African man.

This victory in 1882 by Muoyjang or Dinka People of Aweil was a big setback for the Arab slave traders. They didn't return to Sudan's Aweil region until the second war in 1983, more than a century later. Their defeat convinced Arab traders that the Bar El Gazal Region was closed to slave trading.

My grandfather was celebrated for his leadership and was presented with Commander Abu Meriam's only sword. The village to this day sings a song of praise for Deng Kuol's bravery. His family, which includes his children and their descendants from his five wives, every year celebrates the memories of the sword of Deng Kuol and his 1882 victory over Arab slave traders in Korok, Bour Raal, the Aweil Region of South Sudan.

As Deng Kuol's grandson, I am very grateful for my grandfather's heroism as represented by the sword. The courage and valor he exemplified have shown themselves through many generations and I am here today because of his successful struggle for justice.

My father was Gai Deng Kuol better known as Gai Deng Aduol. I don't have memories of him but his premonition, which prompted him to nickname me Bol Akonyhok before his death, had a major impact on my life. I so thank God for his influence. My father died three months after I was born from blood clots that resulted from a leg wound in battle.

My father's death meant that my oldest brother, Makuach Gai Deng took responsibility for caring for our entire family of four boys and nine girls.

I was the baby of the family so it was my mother, Amiir Dau Akol, who became my whole world. She was my role model, my champion and my hero. She taught me the African Spiritual faith and how I should live right, according to God's principles within Africa's culture guides. She taught me about kindness, integrity, honesty and humanity. She is responsible for everything I do today. Even in my darkest hours, I never gave up my hope and my faith. It is with this hope that I proceed with the vision that God has entrusted to me. It is a vision of a new South Sudan and a new Sudan with freedom, justice and safety, and watching those principles eventually spread to all of Africa. God wants us to always remember our history and culture which has had such an impact on world history.

I also thank God for my first child, my daughter born in 2014 whom I named after my late mother, Amiir Bol Gai Deng. My daughter is the best gift I could give to my mother based on Muoyjang or Jieng traditional culture.

Chapter 1

AFRICA: THE BEGINNING

In the beginning was the land known as Kush or Cush and "Muonyjang" or "Jieng" is the original name of the Kush people. Later it was changed by Arab explorers to "Dinka." While many historical writings about our people have not survived over the centuries, our oral history still keeps our traditions alive to this day.

Our history has always been passed down in our original Muoyjang/Jieng language, called *"thong Muoyjang"* which in English means "human language" or "language of human" in Muoyjang or Jieng. Muoyjang is one of the Neolithic Nile Valley languages along with Shilluk, Nuer, and Luo.

The Jieng's faith begins with God creating the earth. The first human male was called Garang and the first female was named Abuk. Their first child was named Deng. These first humans were created in the land of Kush which today encompasses South Sudan and Sudan.

Kush was an ancient African civilization that can be traced archaeologically back as far as 3000 BC. The kingdom's name comes from the Old Testament Cush, son of Ham, who settled in Northeast Africa. It is mentioned numerous times by among others, the prophets Isaiah and Ezekiel in the Bible.

Head of Kush Ruler ca 716-702 BC , Courtesy of Brooklyn Museum

It should be noted that our Kush/Dinka oral history does not stand alone here. Professor E. E. Evans-Pritchard seems to affirm a Hebrew connection with the Dinka as well as the Nuer (Naath) religions in his 1956 "The Nuer Religion." He postulates that the Nuer and Dinka religions are quite unlike typical "Nilotic" religions and "have features which bring to mind the Hebrews of the Old Testament." He cites others of his time, including Professor C. G. Seligman and American Presbyterian missionary Ms. Ray Huffman, as making similar observations.[3]

The *New World Encyclopedia* also notes:

"...while knowledge of Kush begins from contact with Egypt, the culture predates and may actually have initially stimulated Egyptian culture, not vice versa. Legend has it that the Kush were the oldest race on earth and Nubia is regarded by some as the location of the Garden of Eden. The Biblical description of the Garden of Eden refers in the Hebrew to the land of Cush, usually translated as Ethiopia... women played a key role within the governance of the (Kush) Kingdom, almost unique in the ancient world. A rich and vibrant trading culture, it lived for centuries at peace with neighbors..."[4]

French researcher and writer Antoine Gigal in her article *"Egypt Before the Pharaohs"* at *gigalresearch.com*, further adds:

> "French Egyptologist Emile Amélineau's (1850-1915) excavations in the south of Egypt discovered evidence of the existence of already advanced people earlier than the Pharaohs of the first dynasty. He discovered in particular the people of black race, the Anu (sometimes called "Aunu"). They raised livestock and practiced extensive agriculture all along the Nile and protected themselves inside the defensive walls of cities. They founded the towns of Esna (Anu Tseni), Erment (Anu Menti), Qush, Gebelein (Anti) and even Heliopolis (which was originally named "Anu").
>
> According to many researchers, the greatest figures of ancient Egypt, such as Osiris, Isis, Hermes and Horus came from this ancient Anu race... the Anu knew the use of metals and ivory, they were very organized and knew how to write."[5]

In *"The Egyptian Sudan,"* author J. Kelley Giffen writes in 1902 that Egyptian expert Sir William Flinders Petrie,* after finding an intact, green-glazed pottery tile in the mud around the Abydos temple that contained the name and drawing of the Anu Chief, believed it indicated that "the Sudan question is as old as the beginning of history."[6]

Swiss archaeologist Charles Bonnet, who has spent more than four

---

Petrie is known as the 'Father of Pre-history' for the thousands of books and articles on his excavations in the late 1800's and early 1900s. Giffen was quoting from Petrie's 1902 article in Harper's magazine.

decades in the area told the *New York Times* in 2013: "I discovered a Nubian city in Dukki Gel with original African architecture from around 1500 BC, and in a cache we found 40 pieces of seven monumental statues of pharaohs."

The *Times* reports:

> "In late 2012, he (Bonnet) found what he believes are the city's walls. At the height of its military power around 750 BC, the ancient Kingdom of Kush in northern Sudan ruled over Egypt and Palestine, inaugurating what historians calls the rule of the 25th dynasty and the black pharaohs."

Nubian Pharaohs
Courtesy: Wufei07 24 Jul 2010

Pyramids in Sudan
Courtesy: Mametsaru, 26 Jun 2017

The *Times* concludes:

> "Sudan conjures images of war, instability, drought and poverty. All of those things exist here, often in tragic abundance. But lost in the narrative are the stories of the ancient kingdoms of Kush and Nubia that once rivaled Egypt, Greece and Rome."[7]

Chapter 2

KUSH TO SUDAN: THE MOVE TO ARAB DOMINATION

The experts cited in the previous chapter clearly show that Arabs are not indigenous to Africa. They have unearthed evidence that civilization began in Kush or Nubia in the heartland of Southern Sudan. The ancient Greeks made note of the Kush/Nubian culture and held them in high esteem, describing them as "the holiest and most beautiful of human beings." They called the entire African continent Ethiopia from the Greek word *aithiops* meaning "burnt face," since they thought the Africans looked like people who had been burned by the sun.

This early Ethiopia is often confused with the current country Ethiopia, which is the former Abyssinia, an empire that existed for more than 800 years, from circa 1137 (beginning of Zagwe Dynasty) until 1974 when the Ethiopian monarchy was overthrown in a coup d'etat. The Ethiopian Empire spans a geographical area of today's Ethiopia, Eritrea and Djibouti, and included parts of Northern Somalia, Southern Egypt, Eastern Sudan, Yemen and Western Saudi Arabia.[8] Abyssinia was renamed Ethiopia in the early 1940s.

Kush preceded Ethiopia and Nubia civilizations and all were in existence well before the Arabs invaded from Egypt in 651 AD:

> Following the collapse of the Kingdom of Kush during the 4th century BC, a political vacuum was left in the region it controlled, now modern day Sudan and southern Egypt. This void was filled by the emergence of a number of smaller Nubian kingdoms. The most well-known of these successor states was the Kingdom of Dongola, or Makuria, which had its capital in the city of Old Dongola, located on the east bank of the Nile.

According to Ancient-origins.net:

> "One of the most distinct features of the Kingdom of Dongola is that it was a Christian Kingdom. It is recorded that during the 6th century BC, Christianity was propagated in the Nile Valley from Aswan all the way south to the confluence of the White Nile and the Blue Nile at modern day Khartoum. The Byzantine missionaries were responsible for the spread of Christianity in this region."

The site explains that Byzantine writers recorded the history of the three later kingdoms that followed the Kush Kingdom:

> "Nobatia, Makuria and Alwa (the southern-most state), all of which were converted to Christianity. Whilst Nobatia and Makuria were united, Alwa remained a separate state of its own, perhaps until the beginning of the 16th century."[9]

Arab General Amr Ibn al-'As* came to Egypt in 639 to assist in overthrowing the Roman rulers and conquer the Egyptian blacks. His armies remained to fill the power vacuum and from their fortress in Cairo began, through religion and warfare, to take over much of the rest of Egypt.

The people fought the invading Arab armies but they were unrelenting. A treaty in 751 allowed relative peace but this respite also gave the Arabs time to stealthily push their agenda into powerful Makuria and creep further into the territories, eventually taking over Nobatia.

---

*According to Wikipedia, Amr ibn al-'As, initially anti-Muslim, converted in 629. He was born in Mecca, Arabia and belonged to the nobility of the Quraysh. Like the other Quraysh chiefs, he opposed Islam in the early days but going into battle against the Muslims, he was intrigued by their religious practices and soon converted. He's described as extremely intelligent, a contemporary of Islam's founder, Muhammad, and rose quickly through the ranks to become Commander in Chief of the Muslim Armies in Egypt. He also served as Egypt's governor and is said to have built the first mosque in Africa. He died in 664.[10]

Dongola, Markuria's capital had become solidly Christian as early as the 5th century AD. The ancient Kingdoms of Nobatia and Alodia were also Christian. The Makurian Kingdom remained strong for 400 years but with Arabs in control of Egypt to the north, the Christian Kingdoms were frequently under attack. This virtually continuous assault on Africa's northern regions finally forced them under the Islamic umbrella.

European slave owners did not intermingle with their slaves but Arab men throughout history and today use rape against African women and girls, their off-spring are then indoctrinated into their fathers' Islamic religion. Now, hundreds of years later, these mixed African/Arab descendants are fighting to gain further domination over their African grandparents' people and lands.

South Sudan is under severe pressure as it desperately tries to hold out against international Arab-supported groups seeking to maintain and extend their domination. South Sudanese President Salva Kiir's 2018 bid to join the Arab Union and his newly-signed September 2018 peace agreement with rival Riek Machar brokered by Islamic Sudan and Uganda are just the latest moves in this direction.[11]

President Kiir for years helped lead the Southern rebels fighting against Arab oppression. In his determination to retain power, Kiir now seeks to ally with the Arab League going against his largely Christian, African population.* He doesn't hide his new pro-Sudan agenda to hand over his country to Islamic terror organizations. A June 2018 video posted on Facebook shows South Sudan's Vice President Taban Deng Gai speaking in Arabic insisting that Muslims must have ownership of Christian South Sudan.[12]

*The Arab Union said South Sudan asked to join the Arab Union but was turned down. South Sudan said it hadn't sought membership status but asked to be an "observer." The September 2018 peace agreement is discussed in Chapter 12.

Kiir's lust for power overwhelms his knowledge of history. In the early 1940s, Emperor Haile Selassie officially changed the name of his country Abyssinia. The Emperor chose 'Ethiopia', the name the Greeks' had earlier given to all of the African continent. Prior to Ethiopia it was known as Axum.

Emperor Selassie had taken power in 1916 from his cousin, who favored Islam, a position which proved untenable for the Christian majority in Abyssinia. They never forgot that twelve hundred years earlier the Ethiopian people had welcomed Muslims for protection against their Arab enemies. Ethiopia has been under constant threat from Islamic forces ever since.

Discoveries by Sir Petrie, other researchers and soldiers in the late 1800s revealed wrecked civilizations from Arab invasions going back centuries. They unearthed bits and pieces from great Nile River kingdoms including monuments to their achievements. All were ruins, destroyed by Arab armies in their slow, deliberate march across the continent.

Ethiopian villages were plundered by Arabs who abducted thousands of people then sold them into slavery as laborers and soldiers. British ships patrolled the Indian Ocean throughout the 1800s to prevent human trafficking from Africa. America fought a bloody civil war in the 1860s to outlaw slavery. A decade later, Great Britain was still working to end slavery in Africa and China. The British sent Generals Charles George Gordon, William Hicks, and Herbert Kitchener to the Nile Valley where Khedive Ismail Pasha, leader of the Anglo-Egypt pact, appointed General Gordon to be Governor of Sudan.

Sudanese Arabs strongly resented British interference and did all they could to undermine it. The British, meantime, began organizing and training African troops to help fight for their own liberation.

In the midst of this, an Arab Islamic holy teacher was making a name for himself in Sudan. Muhammad Ahmad was an unusually intelligent, deeply pious zealot who used the chaos to attract a following. He denounced the government for corrupting their faith and insulting the Prophet and called for a restoration of true Islam. In 1881 Ahmad proclaimed himself Mahdi, called adherents to jihad, or holy war, and kicked off an Islamic revolution. The fanatical al-Mahdi was very clever politically, and his writings quickly spread word of his victories. His power and support mushroomed.

Alarmed at last by al Mahdi's success, Egyptian leaders called in Governor Gordon to quell the rebellion but except for a few thousand remaining troops, Gordon was left to do it on his own.

As Giffen tells it, "The story of Gordon's attempt to save Sudan was a pathetic one. We find him making the city of Khartoum his headquarters, then hemmed in on all sides until at last, wholly cut off from the outside world."

Islamic Cleric Muhammad Ahmad
(1844-1885) {{PD-old}}

Death of General Gordon at Khartoum
By Ferris, Jean Leon Gerome,
1863-1930, artist [Public domain]

British General Charles George Gordon
by Geruzet Frères. {PD-1923}

Giffen goes on to describe Gordon "bravely standing to his post, the only Englishman in the city trying to do the work of a hundred men." The dire situation affected his officers, though Gordon inspired them to "resistance for 321 days." Finally, Giffen writes of a "night attack on the palace"… and in late January 1885 Gordon was killed at his Khartoum headquarters, becoming the first European man in Africa to be beheaded.[13]

Since al Mahdi, the Arabs have been working to impose his vision of a caliphate, which is an area that is under the absolute control of Islam and where strict Sharia law is practiced. Arab Muslims have perfected their tactics over the centuries. First they change the language and names. For example, the kingdom of Kush became Sudan. 'Sudan' is Arabic for "land of the black [slave]."

Changing African names and forcing Africans to speak Arabic as I was forced to do in the camps, has been a clever psychological practice.

Naming has always been important among the Muoyjang. Women usually have names that begin with the letter 'A', like Abuk, Achai, Anyang, Akuol, Agum, and Awuor; however, about one percent of the women have names that start with 'N', like Nyibol, Nyandeng, Nyanalaak, and Nyanjok.

Other alphabets do not apply to the Muoyjang women. The names have three meanings: to *Praise God*, *God Given*, and *God Taken*. Most of the other Neolithic groups like Nuer, and Shilluk have women's names beginning with letter 'N'.

Sudan's government has and continues to do everything it can to cloud Africans understanding of their history. As noted earlier, Bol and all students were forced to speak only Arabic during their classes. All students, many unbeknownst to their parents, are also given new Arabic names when they enter school. Their registration and graduation certificates carry only their Arab names so thereafter they must use that name in any legal procedure involving the state.

Language and South Sudan's Revolutionary War 1956-1983

The African Sudanese Revolutionaries in the South were trapped by this successful Arab tactic. The South failed to gain world support because it did not understand how to adequately explain its rebellions against Arab occupation in Sudan. Africans called them 'Anyanya One' and 'Anyanya Two.' Anyanya One in 1956 and Anyanya Two in 1983 did not describe the terrible horrors of Arab enslavement, gang rapes and murders of African people who gave their lives to fight Islam's determination to plant its empire in the heart of Africa.

Arabs are master marketers and to this day call the violence a "civil war" in Sudan which allows them to manipulate world opinion and even mislead African people into believing they are fighting against dissidents. This was and *continues to be a war between African and Arab cultures*. It is about Arab Islamists who want now-independent South Sudan's rich land and resources but not her people– and are trying to control the South's riches and perpetuate genocide on the African population.

The slogan of the Sudan People's Liberation Movement (SPLM) was "equality, justice and freedom." The rebels were not rivals for power, they were freedom fighters desperately trying to defend Africans and African interests from racist Arab Muslims who wanted to wipe out all knowledge of the African people. The Muslims' success so far shows that the rest of Africa and the African diaspora are clueless about the Arab grab for land and control of Africa.

The world must appreciate Africa's true history and respect Africa and her traditions. Africans cannot forge relationships with those who consider themselves masters and have the right to enslave the African people. This is the essence of this centuries-old battle.

The land of Kush existed before Islam; the people of Nubia/Kush are the oldest nation and are the mothers of African continent. The South Sudanese and the marginalized regions of Sudan where many black populations live have suffered the worst crimes against humanity. World leaders must realize that Arab Muslims have no respect for *any* African be they *Muslim or Christian.*

Humanitarian groups and the world community have recorded numerous examples in recent years of Sudan's persecution of the Africans in Darfur who are Muslim, and the vicious attacks on both Muslims and Christians in South Kordofan. Arab Sudanese Muslims preach hatred against African Sudanese regardless of the religion they practice; they describe our people as *Abed* meaning "enslaved."

Bol notes that his adopted hometown of Richmond, Virginia and many others in the American south are in the midst of a controversy over monuments and schools named for Confederate generals from America's Civil War.

Richmond Mayor Levar Stony believes that "African American children should not be walking into schools that are named after those who did not want them to be educated."[14] Where is this same African-American concern for their brothers and sisters in Africa who today are still forced into slavery by Arab Sudanese in the name of Islam? Who are forced to change their names to Arabic if they want to eat or go to school? Too many African-Americans blindly follow the likes of Nation of Islam founder Louis Farrakhan. Too many black inmates in America's prisons and elsewhere are beguiled into the Islamic life. Learn your real history—do not become victim to this insane masochism!

Chapter 3

SUDAN, JIHAD AND OSAMA BIN LADEN

The murderous ways of the Sudanese Jihadi are the same as ISIS, Boko Haram or Al Qaeda; they all preach subjugation and killing in the name of Allah. I first saw this on our march to Dhein when I was seven years old. South Sudanese have dealt with radical Islam since my grandfather's day, but the marginalized areas of Sudan including Darfur, Abyei, Blue Nile, and Nubia Mountains have suffered for centuries. We know well the struggles of our Nubian brothers and sisters. Their indoctrination has been so thorough that many African ethnic groups are fighting for *Arab* and *Islamic* identity after being successfully taught to despise their own *African* identity.

Arabs have convinced many Africans that Islam is superior to any other religion and that to be next to Allah they must ignore their own history and change their ways to Arabic ways beginning with language, dress and lifestyle.

Arabs have been trying to add Sudan to their north African Arab countries since 639 AD. They have not succeeded because resistance of African people in Sudan has been strong as illustrated by my grandfather's story. Today, the Kush Democratic Majority Party and others' education efforts have been making progress among all groups of African Sudanese. Africans must learn that Arabs have never cared about the welfare of Africans. Arabs covet the *vast resources* of Africa. Unless there are substantial changes, North African countries' membership in the African Union will do nothing but smooth the way for the Arab League's conquest of the African people.

The al Madhi's 1881 Revolution in Sudan was inspired by 18th century Wahhabism practiced in what is now modern day Saudi

Arabia. It a strict, puritanical form of Islam that practices Sharia law and governs all aspects of everyday life. Wahhabis believe that Islam should rule the world and all infidels should be converted or dominated. It, by its very core, makes it impossible for lovers of freedom to maintain relationships and democracy.

Wahhabi adherents believe that women are inferior to men, to be treated as commodities and that women, especially African women, are to be dominated. They are required to be completely covered when they venture in public and only then while under the escort of a man. Such beliefs go against the African tradition of women as partners and complements of men. African women have always been held in such esteem that dozens of African queens ruled at one time or another in ancient African civilizations. Nowhere is this seen in Islamic countries.

The flowing Islamic robes made famous by the late Osama bin Laden and that he enforced as the dress code in Sudan are used by terror groups across the Middle East and Africa. It is also the same form of dress adopted by the al Mahdi during his Revolution to crush Sudanese Africans in 1881.

Ironically, it was just over a hundred years later that this new successor to Al-Mahdi with world-wide ambitions to restore the glory of Islam was moving into Sudan and creating a central focus point that would appeal to millions of Muslims all over the world.

Sudan and Osama bin Laden

The late Osama bin Laden came to Sudan from Saudi Arabia where he was born in the late 1950s in Riyadh, the pampered son of a wealthy Yemeni immigrant businessman. The 17th of 57 children, bin Laden stayed close to home and was educated in radical Islamic ideas at King Abdul-Aziz University in Jeddah.

He didn't join the family business, instead signing on with the Islamic Muslim Brotherhood. The Soviets' invasion of Afghanistan in 1979 gave his extreme ideology an outlet and, using his wealth and connections, bin Laden moved to Pakistan and became a fundraiser and recruiter for the Mujahedeen. The experience only served to exacerbate his pro-Islamic ambitions. He founded Al Qaeda in 1988 and went into the terrorism business, deciding to focus on single, high-impact acts of terror instead of a broader military operation.

He returned home after the Afghan/Soviet war but his radical views soon caused problems for the Saudi royal family. Relations worsened after they rejected bin Laden's offer for help after the Iraqi invasion of Kuwait, turning to the US instead. Furious and eventually stripped of his citizenship, in 1991 bin Laden moved his base of operations to the more militant Sudan.

Five weeks after the 9/11 attacks, the *New York Times* reported on a three-year-old federal indictment which charged that Osama bin Laden set up a headquarters for Al Qaeda in Khartoum, Sudan's capital, in 1991, together with numerous companies intended to 'provide income and support' for the terrorist network. The indictment also said al Qaeda had forged alliances with the National Islamic Front, the ruling party in Sudan.[15]

The Independent UK article on Osama bin Laden
by Robert Fisk, Monday, December 6, 1993.

The *East African* reported in 2011 that US Judge John Bates ruled that "Sudanese intelligence and military officials provided "support and protection" for those directly involved in the (1998 Embassy) bombings... the assistance included "hundreds of Sudanese passports" as well as arrangements for al Qaeda members to "travel over the Sudan-Kenya border without restriction, permitting the passage of weapons and money to supply the Nairobi terrorist cell."[16]

The *Times* report continues noting that Sudan's ruling National Islamic Front also went after the South's oil fields:

> Nongovernmental organizations and international monitors have said that the government and its allies have used campaigns of violence and terror to clear civilians away from oil fields, with the witting or unwitting support of Talisman (a Canadian company with oil and gas operations in Sudan) and its partners.[17]

Talisman defended its Sudanese investment and called the charges unfair.

James Astill of *The Guardian* reports bin Laden's millions were a most welcome addition to Sudan, a poor country ravaged by violence after Omar al-Bashir's military coup in 1989 ousting a democratically-elected President. In his five years there, bin Laden set up several businesses, including a huge construction company and a farm where he planted thousands of acres of crops.[18]

Meanwhile, the Sudanese government, which had declared a *jihad* against the country's Christian rebels, was augmenting the army with Islamist militias, forcibly enlisted from Khartoum's sandy streets and souks. Bin Laden is rumored to have been funding them heavily.

Osama bin Laden revealed a little of this in a rare interview in 1993 with Robert Fisk of the UK *Independent*:

> "Yes, I helped some of my comrades to come here to Sudan after the war.' How many? Osama Bin Laden shakes his head. 'I don't want to say. But they are here now with me, they are working right here, building this road to Port Sudan.'... Thus did Mr. bin Laden reflect upon *jihad* while his former fellow combatants looked on. Was it not a little bit anti-climactic for them, I asked, to fight the Russians and end up road-building in Sudan? 'They like this work and so do I. This is a great plan which we are achieving for the people here, it helps the Muslims and improves their lives."[19]

This is the point Bol Gai Deng makes as well. It was *Muslims* bin Laden worked to help. For Sudan's Christians, his *help* cost many their lives. Young Bol Gai Deng began to personally feel the effects of bin Laden's influence in Sudan. After Bol's earlier serendipitous escape from his Arab owner by hopping a train to Khartoum, he was led by fellow Dinka to a refugee camp. For months, he spent his days in lessons, though only in Arabic, as required by Sudanese President Omar al-Bashir.

Bashir had somewhat tolerated churches and Christian schools in Sudan until bin Laden's influence prompted a crackdown there as well. Churches began to be shuttered and students became prisoners in their schools.

Soldiers went from building to building capturing classmates, killing many but others were forced into the military or servitude. Bol was able to escape again thanks to a Pastor who helped him and several other students get out of Khartoum and on their way to Egypt. (Despite many hardships in Egypt, it was there that Bol was able to get the attention of UN and US officials and move to Richmond, Virginia.)

Meantime, in Sudan, bin Laden's hatred of the United States grew, as he continued his strategy of uniting various terror groups to take their fight directly to the only superpower still standing. He set up a training camp on his property near Khartoum and began to build teams for terror acts at many identified American targets. From al Qaeda's first 1992 bombing of a Yemeni hotel that just missed US peacekeeping troops to arming Somalis who killed 18 American servicemen in Mogadishu, and training the mastermind of the World Trade Center bombing, both in 1993, Al Qaeda was making its mark. Astill concludes that "Bin Laden's years in Sudan were crucial for the development of his terrorist network."[20]

Counterterrorism expert, author and former Ambassador Daniel Benjamin believes that bin Laden's success came because he "cast his agenda as springing from religious — rather than political — motivations. Bin Laden is a deeply pious man, Benjamin said. And to top it off, he had the money and fundraising skills to finance his ambitions.

"So he really reshaped the struggle. He's managed to create both an authentic cause, an authentic ideology, and to find the means to carry it out," Benjamin said. "And I fear that the path that he hewed, he cut, is one that others are going to travel for some time to come."[21]

Bol Gai Deng shares Ambassador Benjamin's fear when it comes to his beloved South Sudan:

"My warning is clear: the aim of the minority Arab Sudanese, with money obtained from various international Islamic sources, is still to take over as much of Africa as they can. This is why Africa must begin to assert its true identity and resist total destruction. The Saudi Arabian Islamic pattern that bin Laden championed, is now seen in many circles in Africa. This is the major, absolute, and present danger.

If we do not know our history, we are bound to repeat the mistakes of the past. We see what is happening in Sudan and we know that President Al-Bashir is using this same formula to frighten, scare and kill the people of Darfur, Nubia, Blue Nile, South Kordofan, and South Sudan regions."

Chapter 4

PERSECUTION OF THE MARGINALIZED PEOPLE OF SUDAN

Morningstar News reports that persecution against Christians by the Arab Islamic government in Khartoum has intensified since South Sudan's succession in 2011.

Two years later, government officials announced that "no new licenses would be granted for building new churches in Sudan" because of a dwindling Christian population.

Morningstar says Sudan has also expelled foreign Christians, bulldozed church buildings, raided Christian bookstores and arrested Christians. "Authorities threatened to kill South Sudanese Christians who do not leave or cooperate with them in their effort to find other Christians." the news site reported.[22]

Pastors Hassan Abdelrahimahim Tawor and Kowa Shamal were among several ministers and mission workers arrested by the Khartoum government. They were charged with espionage, causing hatred and spreading false information through their Christian work. We met with Pastors Tawor and Shamal in December 2017 in Richmond, Virginia. Rev. Tawor told us that they were put in very tough prisons run by Sudan's Secret police and held for five months. "My family knew nothing about what happened and rumors were that we were dead. We were beaten, interrogated about the church and mission activities, and then put into cells."

Pastor Tawor said that at one prison he was one of 37 prisoners who were put into a cell the size of a small conference room. "We slept lined up head to foot and we were in that room for three months, sleeping on the floor, Tawor said. Finally, they were taken to court, "

"A lot of Christians were at the court," Tawor said, "singing songs to show they were standing with their pastors. The government was shocked at the number of people who stood with us. They thought most of the Christians had gone to the South and they were here and were singing—a powerful presentation," he remembered.

Rev. Tawor said that the prosecutor was supposed to spell out the charges but the singing was so loud—they were singing about David and Goliath—that he (the prosecutor) fell out of his chair. The government was shaking and fearing that something would happen." After a seven-month-trial, he and several other ministers were sentenced to 12 years in prison. A Czech minister, Peter Yesick, was sentenced to 24 years.

The Christian prisoners didn't know it but across the world social media was helping to create a growing awareness of the persecution. Facebook posts caught the attention Flanna Garrett, the wife of newly-elected Virginia Congressman Tom Garrett (R-5th). The couple was touched by the ministers' courage and strength. Flanna had earlier lived in the Czech Republic for five to six years so hearing about Rev. Yesick hit home to her. She asked her husband to get involved.

Congressman Garrett had just taken office in January 2017. He told us in a January 2018 meeting in his office that "I didn't know any better…I got in my car and drove over to the Sudanese Embassy and asked to speak with the ambassador." Garrett demanded entry into Sudan and after much communication between human rights organizations, churches and the Sudanese government, Garrett went into Sudan and was able to get Rev. Tawor and another pastor released from prison. Rev. Yesick was released too.

With Garrett's help the Tawor family was allowed to come to Virginia. Garrett's fellow church members, led by Curt and Diana Shores, fixed up a home for the family and raised money to pay for food, clothing and other expenses.

Pastor Tawor said his ministry in Sudan focused on helping church members prepare for possible persecution. "Constitutionally we have freedom of religion but in reality the government wants to break the church. (Sudan President) Bashir is Muslim. Arab Muslims run the country in Sudan... Arabs who came from the Middle East."

The Sudanese Islamic government's attempts to stop Christian outreach backfired just as the imprisonment of the Apostles did two thousand years ago. "We preached the gospel to prisoners, including the Muslims," Rev. Tawor said, "prisoners who were going to [be] hung or have their hands cut off. Some were Christian, some were Muslim. We prepared them for whatever was going to happen to them," Tabor added.[23]

Persecution isn't just confined to African Christians. Nazar Suliman grew up in an African Muslim family in the Nubian Mountains. Now a US citizen, Nazar spent a year and a half imprisoned in an Egyptian jail for his protests against the persecution of the Nubian Mountain people.

Once in the United States, Nazar founded a group of refugees from the Nubian Mountain region that has more than ten thousand members. He has spent much of his time trying to bring awareness to the persecution of his people. Nazar believes it is time for Africans of every faith to join together and bring change not only to South Sudan but the people of Nubian Mountains, Blue Nile, Darfur, and Abyei. His hope is that the people in the marginalized areas of Sudan will finally be allowed, as promised by the Comprehensive Peace Agreement, to vote on whether to join the country of South Sudan.

Chapter 5

AFRICANS MUST UNITE AND PROTECT THEIR HISTORY

The African diaspora in the United States, Brazil, Colombia, France, England, Canada, the Caribbean, and those throughout the African continent must understand and respond to threats to the very lives and cultures of African people. Sudan is the front line of this struggle.

They need to understand that Arab racists in the name of Islam were the first to introduce slavery in Africa and for centuries they have been able to hide behind the more obvious European slave trade while continuing their own enslavement of Africans far longer than Europeans—and are actively engaged in human trafficking even now. I was abducted and sold at the age of seven to an Arab master. I know this first hand.

Africans abroad clearly see the white man's history of slave trading but many do not see ongoing Arab sales of human beings, destroying African families and culture. In Sudan, the Arab League protects Arab leaders but no one, not even the African Union, protects Africans. Arab leaders are always pushing Africans south and away from the rich Nile River Valley to make room for Arabs from Africa and the Middle East.

The African Union must realize that radical Islam covers for Arab racism and poses an imminent danger to Somalia, Niger, Chad, Mali, Senegal and Nigeria. The Arab Project is not simply to spread the Muslim faith but to Arabize as much of Africa as it can.

The United States of Africa was the vision of 1950s and 60s revolutionaries including Kwame Nkrumah. When Ghana gained independence from Britain in 1957, Nkrumah vowed that "Ghana's independence is meaningless unless it is linked up with the total liberation of the African continent." This is not any Arabs' vision for Africa. They are pursuing the example set by Mohammad Ahmad when he kicked off his Islamic revolution in 1881.[24] He was already a major slave trader, sending out forces to capture thousands of Africans to take to the Arab slave markets of El-Obeid, Dongola, Bat al-Mal.

After Mahdi's death his followers formed the Umma Party in 1945 to continue his work. The Mahdi's great-great-grandson Al-Sadiq Al-Mahdi currently heads the Umma party. Mohammed Ahmad al-Mahdi and his descendants are the ones who have plotted to take over Africa's rich lands. They must be blamed for the 1987 Dhein massacre mentioned earlier in the Introduction. More than a thousand Dinka were killed in a weekend massacre by Rizeigat Arab militias, backed by the Sudanese government, in the Southern Darfur province on March 28, 1987. Some Dinka were killed in a church, others were under police protection, many were told they were going to be moved for their safety and loaded onto five trains where they were killed. Ushari Ahmed Mahmud and Suleyman Ali Baldo say that the number listed as dead is a conservative figure. Their investigation of the Dhein massacre is reported in their book *Human Rights Abuses in Sudan in 1987.*[25]

Sudanese Who Inspire

Why did Africans forget their ancestors? How have so many Africans been converted to Islam? Arab enslavers used force, terror and propaganda to browbeat many Africans into submission. Not all bowed under, including my grandfather and the Jieng people. There are examples of brave fighters against Arabization both historically and in our present.

The Sudanese trace a glorious past to the dawn of civilization and the kingdoms of Meroe and Kush. *National Geographic History* magazine noted the shaping of these early cultures:

> Kushite culture blended Egyptian customs into its own, creating a distinctive, visual style. Truncated and with steep sides, the pyramids left by the long line of Nubian kings populate the desert near the site of Meroë.

NGH reporter Núria Castellano writes, "The center of a powerful civilization, Meroë served as the capital city of Kush whose robust culture thrived for centuries. Their grand architecture and works of art left a lasting testament to the greatness of the Nubian kings and queens." Castellano calls the pyramids "perhaps their grandest achievements" noting that with more than 200 built at Meroe, Sudan has "more pyramids than all of Egypt."

With access to mines and minerals, the Meroites were expert gold workers. While we don't know their names, their legacy includes not only the exquisite pyramids, but also temples, palaces, and royal baths in their capital.[26]

Journalist Henry T. Aubin, in his painstakingly researched book, *The Rescue of Jerusalem*, outlines a historical political/military achievement. It involves an alliance between Hebrews and Africans in 701 BC which set up what he termed "one of history's more heroic exploits."

> "The Kushites, or Nubians… lived in what is now northern Sudan and southernmost Egypt. In the late eighth century BC a king of Kush took control of all of Egypt, right up to the Mediterranean and formed its 25th Dynasty. For two generations Kush was among the most powerful nations anywhere in the Mediterranean world. Of the total of 31 Dynasties [of ancient Egypt]… there is one which all historians… agree was black… that dynasty is the 25th."

Aubin's research found a "fleeting mention of a military expedition that a Kushite pharaoh in 701 BC had dispatched to the Near East… which corresponds to today's Israel. Its aim: to prevent an Assyrian conquest of Jerusalem. Aubin writes that he was riveted by the black pharaoh's action:

> "Never have I heard of Black-African forces in ancient times journeying outside the continent. Also, never have I seen evidence that seemed to refute so strongly certain extremists' anti-Semitic claim, which was then attracting considerable publicity, that blacks and Hebrews had been adversaries throughout history. The Kushites' long-distance attempt to save the Hebrew capital, Jerusalem, implied a strong alliance between these two peoples."

He reports that the "Kushites' intervention came when the powerful Assyrian army laid siege to Jerusalem after pillaging 46 Judean towns and cities, torturing and executing their leaders."

Aubin argues, the Kush army enabled the fragile, war-torn Hebrew kingdom to survive and nurse itself back to economic and demographic health, thereby allowing the Hebrew religion, Yahwism, to evolve within the next several centuries into Judaism of which later grew two great offshoots, Christianity and Islam.

Thus, Aubin says, the Kushite's Jerusalem mission "set off a series of events that have helped define religion in the West and have determined the course of history.

Without the Kushites' role in 701 BC, then, the world would have become inconceivably different."[27]

Achievements extend to modern times such as in the life of Josephine Margret Bakhita, (ca. 1869-1947). Bakhita was born in Darfur, a member of the historic Daju people, and niece of the village chief. Her father was also considered very successful. Bakhita's happy childhood was very similar to Bol and thousands of other Sudanese children. Her peaceful life was shattered in February 1877 when she was kidnapped by Arab slave traders, the same attackers who had taken her elder sister two years earlier. Bakhita was forced to walk barefoot to the El-Obeid slave market and sold twice on the way. Between 1877 and 1889 she was sold three more times and then given away, experiences that left her so traumatized she could not even remember her name. The slavers called her **Bakhita** which is Arabic for *lucky*. She doubtless realized the irony of that nickname. 'Lucky' Bakhita was also forced to convert to Islam.

She escaped to Italy in 1885 with her new owner the Italian Vice Consul in Khartoum, who treated her cordially. She was sold again, however, before an Italian court ruled that Sudan had outlawed slavery before she was born so, as slavery was not recognized in Italy, she was legally free and her own person. Those who knew her said her "mind was always on God and her heart on Africa."[28] She became a nun in Italy and served until her death in 1947. The Catholic Church proclaimed her a saint in the year 2000.

The 21st Century fight for South Sudanese independence is marked by a host of heroes and martyrs to the cause of freedom. Their stories are told in Chapter Six.

Chapter 6

FROM EGYPT TO SUDAN TO SOUTH SUDAN

The Arabs took over Egypt and then used it as a base to begin their incursions into Sudan. They diluted the African culture and imposed their own beliefs to wipe out African history. Arabs brought violence, war and sexual slavery. Their attacks on African women over the years produced a race of people who became anti-African (anti-black) who adopted their fathers' Arab superiority and forgot that their mothers' veins flow with the blood of black people. They spoke Arabic because it was the only tongue available to them. Thus they were denied knowledge of their black history because it is passed down orally through the original *"thong Muoyjang"* language.

The Sudanese Arab minority took the reins of power after Sudan's independence in 1956. Their concern continued to be protecting and expanding the Arab control over the native African people. African life was an endless cycle of resistance and struggle.

Independence also allowed the ruling minority to make language and name changes from their domination playbook. "Sudan" is Arabic for "land of the black people." Africans know that the phrase in Arab minds really means: "land of the black slave." This name change itself shows that the Arabs knew that they were on the indigenous land of the African people.

Sudan, before the split, was the biggest country on the continent and is considered the gateway to Africa. The Arab Sudanese are the 'tip of the spear' to finally and completely deprive Africans of their land and culture. They have been patient and determined for centuries. Unless Africans educate themselves quickly, the Arabs' current hold on power foreshadows their eventual success: only

51

Sudanese Arab rulers have controlled Sudan since 1952 and that includes current ruler Omar al-Bashir who took over Sudan in a bloodless coup in 1989.

During these years despite the desperate efforts of SPLM/SPLA, the south suffered tremendous losses. In the 1986 democratic election, 37 of the 68 southern constituencies were not allowed to vote because of what was deemed political unrest. Students in the extremely poor western Sudan had spurred thousands to sometimes violent protests against the lack of food and other necessities of life.

As mentioned earlier, it was in 1987 that a thousand Dinka who had sought refuge were murdered by government-backed militias in Dhein. Similar government-back militias continuously raided and pillaged southern villages, killing men, gang-raping women and kidnapping able-bodied children, including Bol, to sell in Dhein and other northern slave markets.

Africans need to realize that this is part of an overall pattern. It is no accident that all 15 rulers of Sudan over the past 66 years were Muslim Arabs from Northern Sudan with no roots in the traditional cultures or the Christian faith of the majority of the indigenous people. They are the leaders of what is identified as the *Arab Project*.[29] It is their calculated, long-range vision to push out Africans by promoting diaspora. Their successful scattering of Sudanese Africans throughout the world came through their constant attacks on the legitimate rights of the majority Sudanese people. Diaspora would also help eliminate potential future African Sudanese leaders.

Sudanese Africans had a single bright spot in 2011 when, after a long, bitter, and protracted battle, ninety-eight percent of South Sudanese voted for freedom from the North. African Sudanese in South Sudan and all over the world,including Richmond, Virginia, celebrated on July 9th, when South Sudan was declared an independent country.

Their jubilance was short-lived, however. South Sudan won its independence but Arabs immediately began stirring up trouble in the young country. They quickly moved in and purchased land and businesses in Juba, sought to influence the newly-elected and naïve political leaders, and undermined every institution they could in South Sudan. Seven years later, ninety percent of South Sudanese businesses are owned by foreigners. These favored foreigners continuously sow seeds of ethnic and tribal conflict to keep violent chaos churning, so far successfully preventing the 2018 elections which were agreed to in the Comprehensive Peace Agreement.

As Bol Gai Deng predicted in a 2010 article,[30] the South Sudanese government is abetting this effort. In fact, its shadowy history very much resembles what US President Donald Trump would likely describe as a "crooked movement": under-the-radar actions aimed at obfuscating often illegal maneuvers to bring about desired political results and control.

History of South Sudan's Independence

The beginnings of South Sudan's move toward independence gained momentum in 1946 when the British and Egyptian administrators, who had been governing Sudan for 48 years, decided to combine the separate North and South areas into one political region. This was done despite deep Southern fears of being dominated by the politically powerful North. Tensions inevitably grew between the largely Christian South and the predominantly Muslim North. Two years later, the British and Egypt agreed that Sudan should become self-governing and in 1954 Sudan's newly-elected Parliament declared Sudan an independent republic, which became official January 1, 1956.

The Sudan was thereafter administered by a number of different governments and for 27 of the next 37 years was under military rule and, as previously noted, none of the rulers was an indigenous African. Africans know all too well (and history shows) that descendants of Al-Madhi, enemy oppressor of Bol's grandfather's generation, exerted their power over Sudan for many of those years.

An elected coalition government headed by Al-Mahdi's Umma Party and the National Unionist Party took over in 1965 but was toppled four years later by Colonel Jaafar Nimeiri and his troops. Nimeiri abolished existing political institutions and established the Democratic Republic of Sudan with supreme authority vested in a Revolutionary Command Council.

Sudan adopted a permanent constitution, confirmed the president as head of state and commander of the armed forces. The judiciary was made directly responsible to the president. The Sudanese Socialist Union (SSU) was recognized as the sole legal political organization in the country.

The State Security Act was adopted. It created numerous political offences and gives broad powers of search and arrest to the state security services.

Economic conditions had already deteriorated while continued religious frictions, strikes and military-backed suppression of the South's African culture and identity forced thousands of Southern Sudanese to flee to neighboring countries. It proved too much for many soldiers from the South. They defected, including Joseph Lagu, a South Sudanese officer in the North's 10th Brigade. He founded the military wing of the South's first resistance. This resistance, this "war over cultures" lasted for 17 years in which half a million people died. Four out of five who perished were civilians.

Lagu took control of the total Southern resistance in 1971 and the rebellion grew. Nimeiri started secret talks with Lagu and hostilities came to an end in March 1972.

Lagu successfully negotiated the establishment of the South as a self-governing region with equal representation in the South's military and promises there would be no discrimination on the basis of religion, ethnic background, place of birth, tribe or sex.

The agreement brought some relative peace for 10 years. In 1978 Lagu was elected President of the Southern Council or cabinet. He was appointed Sudan's 2nd Vice President in 1982.

Not everyone in the South, however, embraced the 1972 Nimeiri / Lagu peace agreement. Samuel Gai Tut who was from the Nuer tribe and Akout Atem Atem, a Dinka, were leaders of the "Southern Front," and refused to sign on to the peace plan. They went into hiding in the bush for ten years.

Meantime, Chevron discovered oil in 1978 in the southern Sudan area near Bentiu and its rich potential exacerbated what was already a long-running dispute over boundaries. There were debates over where the oil was actually located. Sudan's parliament in 1980 tried to redraw boundaries and annex the oil fields to Kordofan but that plan was withdrawn after protests from the South. Another point of contention was how the oil would be produced.*

Colonel turned President Nimeiri was a socialist and pursued pan-Arabist policies at first, then became an ally of the United States but, over time, pressure from his Islamist opponents forced him to Islam and an alliance with the Muslim Brotherhood. Despite promises to the Christian South ten years earlier, Nimeiri in 1983 imposed Sharia law on the entire country.

Nimeiri was overthrown in a bloodless coup in 1985 led by armed forces chief of staff General Abdel-Rahman Swar al-Dahab. He appointed a 15-member Transitional Military Council (TMC) to rule Sudan, and promised to hold elections in a year. Though the TMC was generally accepted in the North, it faced a skeptical South. Meantime, Sudan's economy was a mess, it faced major debt, industrial output had dropped 50 percent, there were food shortages and famine was on the horizon. By early 1986 the International Monetary Fund declared Sudan bankrupt. Once again, Al-Mahdi's Umma Party moved in.

A change of government didn't help the south. Famine became a southern reality in 1986 claiming an estimated quarter of a million southern Sudanese in 1988 alone. Within a year thousands of starving southerners had moved north in a desperate search for food.

Two Sudanese army officers (and best friends) who had tried to

---

*Discussion of the major, continuing controversy over South Sudan's oil can be found in Chapter 7.

work with Khartoum, rebelled after Nimeiri's imposition of sharia law. This extreme, fundamentalist practice only meant further persecution of southern Christians. Officers William Nyuon Bany and Kerubino Kuanyin Bol went into hiding with fellow South Sudanese and started a second rebellion.

John Garang is widely known as the founder of the SPLM, but at this point he was in the United States, studying for his doctorate at the University of Iowa under a Khartoum scholarship. When he received word of the fighting, he returned to Sudan promising to convince rebel leaders Nyuon and Kerubino to put down their arms and return to their posts. Dr. Garang went into the bush to meet with the rebels but never returned to Khartoum.

Instead he formed an alliance with Nyuon and Kerubino and the Sudan People's Liberation Movement (SPLM), defended by its military arm, the Sudan People's Liberation Army (SPLA) were born. Dr. Garang was chosen as leader out of respect for his high level of education. SPLM/SPLA co-founders Kerubino was named Vice President of the SPLM while Nyuon took control of the SPLA. Garang named fellow Dinka Salva Kiir as head of his security.

Garang's next step was to set up a meeting with the Southern Front's Tut and Atem to unite all the rebels into one opposition party. Somehow the meeting went terribly wrong. The two sides could not agree on two big issues: 1) the Southern Front wanted to fight only for South Sudan and its independence; and 2) the Southern Front favored Atem as leader because he was older and had wisdom born of his extensive experience. The SPLM/SPLA's Dr. Garang was well-educated but young and inexperienced.

Disagreement turned to anger and when the smoke cleared witnesses say, Garang's men had killed both Southern Front's leaders Tut, a Nuer and Atem from the Dinka tribe.

Fear and jealousy are powerful human emotions that can override an effort to promote the common good. Dr. Garang and the other leaders united opposition parties to fight oppression from the North, but the struggle soon gave way to rivalries in both wings leading to abuses. As founding leader, Dr. Garang, with his Security Director Kiir, was determined to keep control. Kiir's job was to eliminate any opposition, much like his brother-in-law Akol Koor does today as President Kiir's Security Services Director.

Some of the early rivals within the SPLM/SPLA who were slain include Benjamin Bol Akok in 1986. Seven years later in 1993 five leaders, all with the first name Martin, were killed on the same day: Martin Majier Gai, Martin Bol Makuang, Martin Kajivora Maina, Martin Makur Aleyou and Martin Manyiel. They had disagreed with parts of Garang's campaign strategy against the North. The victims' family members say that Garang and Kiir feared the five might try to take over the movement so they were eliminated.

Also that same day Bol's personal hero, General Kawac Makuei Mayar, who had successfully recruited and mobilized 85,000 young South Sudanese to the SPLA, was arrested and imprisoned for seven years. Mayar later talked with Bol about Bol's grandfather's legacy and General Mayar annually celebrated Bol's grandfather's victory over Islam. When he died in 2017, Bol and Mayar's daughter organized a special memorial service for the General in Richmond. His daughter lives in Richmond and for 4 years worked as Bol's Secretary of Information in the US Aweil Youth Association (AYA). She is currently Chairman of the Aweil Community Association USA's Richmond Chapter.

As the South's rebellion continued in Sudan, so did the practice of eliminating potential rivals. In 2002, SPLA General George Kuach was poisoned while hospitalized for a gun wound in Nairobi. Community leaders in Nairobi and the General's family say he was killed over his disagreements with Dr. Garang.

The late Dr. Garang described his campaign as a "New Sudan Vision," a version that sought African alliances with dictators, be they Islamist or Communist. This view has been adopted by various African leaders since 1960.

KDMP's vision, championed by Bol Gai Deng, calls for a "United States of Kush" that guarantees equality under the law, government transparency and democratic elections with term limits at the national, regional and local levels, first in South Sudan and then throughout Africa.

Kush Pan Africanism elevates women to equal status and includes individual freedom for all. The Garang and Kiir version employs propaganda over education. KDMP believes an educated people will be able to withstand the lure of peace under authoritarian rule in favor of a free, if messier democratic process. KDMP supporters know first-hand that persecution of minorities is the first step in the path to tyranny for all.

The early Sudan People's Liberation Movement and Army's chaotic beginnings boded ill for the vision of a free and independent South Sudan and continues to divide South Sudan to this day. Garang and Kiir ruled by force through fear and it was inevitable that the freedom-loving Southern Front leaders were eventually eliminated.

In 2005 Dr. Garang lost his life in a helicopter crash. Though it was ruled accidental, some of Kiir's critics still suspect that Garang died by a close rival using Garang's own methods. Kiir, wanting Garang's power, is believed by opponents to have formed an alliance with Uganda's President Yoweri Museveni (discussed further in Chapter 11) and they conspired to cause Garang's fatal crash.

No matter how Garang died, General Salva Kiir moved quickly to benefit from the tragedy and continues to employ the politics of fear and intimidation to maintain control over the country.

Months before Garang's death, the 2005 Comprehensive Peace Agreement had ushered in a power-sharing government, a new constitution and promises of a referendum on the South's independence within six years.

The South was given a large degree of control over its government but deadly clashes continued between the North and South, prompting the rise of numerous rebel groups. Terms of the South's promised independence referendum were worked out in 2009 and in 2011 an overwhelming majority 98% of southern Sudanese voted for independence.

Kiir's pursuit of power in the South, like that of Sudan's Islamic President Bashir, is not derived from a desire to help the people. It is based on greed, on his determination to control the South's substantial wealth through its resources.

In May 2012 "South Sudan's government acknowledged that South Sudanese officials had 'stolen' $4 billion of missing funds that were supposed to go to developing the war-torn state—the equivalent of roughly two entire years of official revenue. Worse, this money was looted directly under the noses of the international community, which agreed to supervise the peace process and even provided consultants to do South Sudan's own bookkeeping."[31]

Meantime, South Sudan's independence left the rest of the Africans in Sudan at the mercy of Bashir's government which has never ceased killing and maiming the people.

The practice of genocide has often been used against small ethnic groups in Sudan. The historic list is long: the Torritt Massacre in 1955, the killing of South Sudanese intellectuals at Wau in 1964, the burning alive of South Sudanese in Babanusa in 1965, the war in Anyanga which ended in 1972, the Massacres of South Sudanese Students in Nyamlel High School in 1983, the Arab Islamic and Sudanese African second war of Anyanya in 1983, the murder of hundreds of South Sudanese inside the five trains in Dhein in 1987 and on and on. One can recount seemingly endless horrors caused in Sudan by the Arab Islamic jihadists whose only ambition is to control Africans and African resources.

The numbers are astonishing and genocide continues today. The Darfurians and Nubians and other people of the country are currently under severe pressure.

Dr. Matthew LeRiche, author, filmmaker and independent analyst wrote in 2013 of meeting large groups of fleeing refugees in Sudan's Blue Nile while on a fact finding mission to Sudan: "The refugees told us their main reasons for fleeing: the consistent aerial bombardments by the Sudanese military, but many were unsure and confused as to why they were being targeted by their own government."

LeRiche said he found the people terrified, starving with very little water. "One community leader said he suspected (Khartoum's attacks) were "because they were simply not the kind of people Sudan's president, Omar al-Bashir, wants in the country — that is, people of deeply African character. Although many share the Islamic faith with those ruling in Khartoum, the people in Blue Nile are considered a thorn in the repressive regime's side because of their historic support for an open, secular, democratic Sudan."[32]

The numbers are sobering: between 1955-1972 one and a half million South Sudanese died at the hands of Khartoum or govern-ment-backed militias. Three million South Sudanese died from 1983 to 2005. One hundred thousand Africans in the North's Nubia Mountains were murdered between 1988 and 2002, genocide in Darfur took between 400,000 to 600,000 lives between 2003 and 2011, and from 2011-2016 more than 150,000 Africans, from Nubia, Blue Nile and Darfur, were slain by Khartoum's Arab racists.

Meantime, enslavement of Africans by Arab Muslims overshadow all others throughout history. The Arab slave trade has lasted 14 centuries and continues to this day in places like Libya, Mauritania, Saudi Arabia, and Sudan.[33]

Arab Islamic slave traders and their descendants (many of whom are themselves part African) have transported nearly 20 million enslaved (mostly black women and children) out of Africa. Another 85 million are believed to have died at sea en route or across the deserts.[34]

January 1, 1956
Line of Demarcation

Courtesy: United Nations - Dept of Field Support

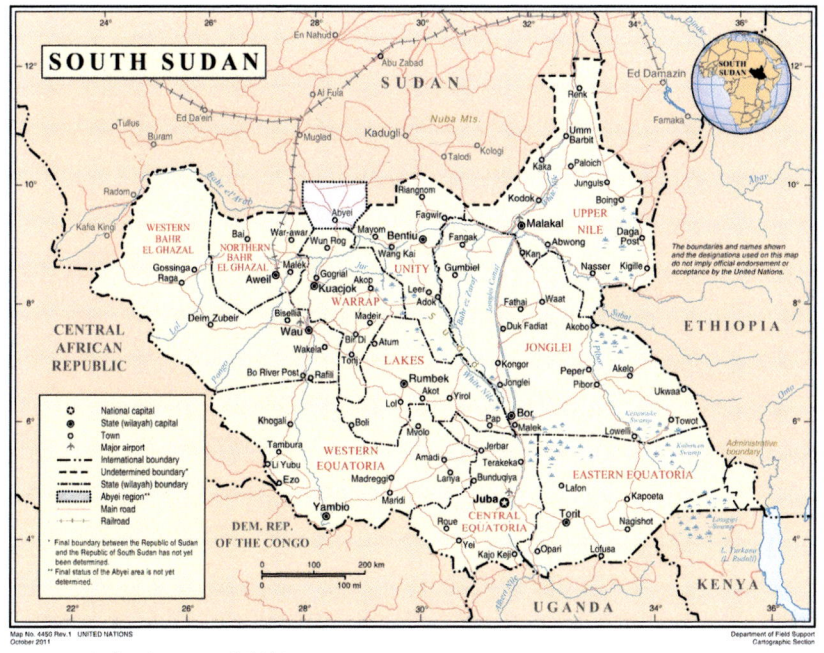

Courtesy: United Nations - Dept of Field Support

Amiir Dau Akol
Bol Gai Deng's late mother

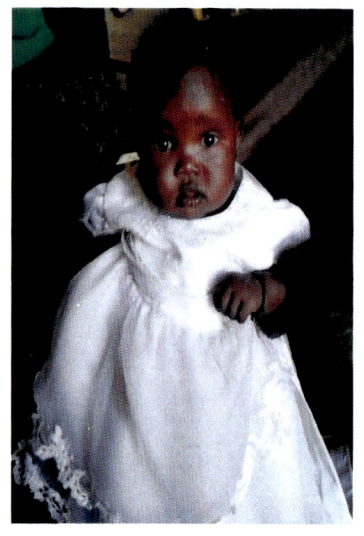

Bol's daughter, Amiir Bol Gai Deng

Bol at his 2008 graduation from Virginia Commonwealth University flanked by his adopted American parents, Jill and the late Frank Wood.

Bol's life in pictures

Courtesy of Michael Hayden, Lutheran World Federation, 2013.

Courtesy: Stuart Prince, Albany Association.

Center right: Janjaweed (armed horseman) like those who raided Bol's village and abducted him when he was 7 years old. Clockwise: Bol spent three years as a slave and still has the scars from chains like these; Bol and friends at Khartoum refugee camp; Sword of Islamic General Hussein Ben Meriam slain by Bol's grandfather in 1882 during the Islamic Revolution. His heroic victory drove out Islam from Aweil, South Sudan for nearly a hundred years and it is still celebrated today; Bol at VCU 2018; South Sudan flag; Bol speaking at 2016 rally in front of the White House; a relaxed Bol at his Richmond home; Childhood education is very important to the Sudanese, even in refugee camps.

A 2007 oil spill in Rabak, Sudan. Photo: Courtesy of UN Environmental Programme.

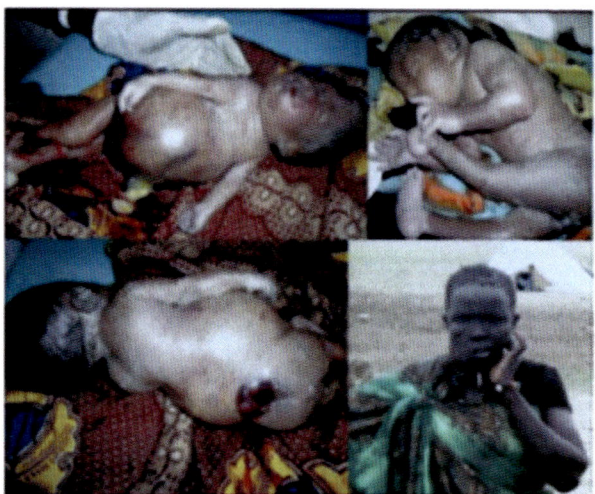
An alarming number of newborn deformities and adult victims of oil pollution near South Sudan oil fields. The government has virtually ignored their plight until recently. Photo Courtesy: of Ruweng State.

Contaminated oil spill/mudslide spreads pollution to nearby farmland and homes, December 2017.
Photo Courtesy: Nile Institute of Environmental Health

South Sudan's Malual Both Anyar dance group welcomes Bol and the KDMP team to Uganda, May 2018.

Nazar Suliman protesting the persecution of the Nuba Mountains people in front of the White House, January 2011.

Bol Gai Deng, Co-founder/Chairman of the Aweil Youth Association USA, 2015

Nazar Suliman and his Nuba Mountains group protest in front of the Egyptian Embassy in Washington, D.C. 2010.

Bol Gai Deng and supporters proudly display the South Sudanese flag after the vote for independence in 2011.

South Sudanese refugees celebrate their country's vote for independence on July 9, 2011 in Richmond, Virginia.

Jul-15-2010 19:27
Can We Afford Another Al-Bashir, in the South?
William Deng for Salem-News.com

Kiir Mayradit is a criminal, he takes advantage of his people and does not allow democracy to flourish, his lack of honor will bring war to our nation when we need peace

(WASHINGTON D.C.) - At great risk to myself and those close to me that are still in Sudan, I have written this letter to bring awareness of what is happening inside the South Sudanese government.

I have already received threatening emails and several friends have been telephoned by those inside the government, in an effort to intimidate.

My belief is the Private Secretary of President Kir is calling and writing emails to pressure me into silence and those, that are strong in their resistance to the tyranny that is President Kiir.

In the South, Sudanese have nothing to eat; Salva Kiir doesn't care about those who are struggling with poverty after they lost their family members in Civil War. We are going to suffer under Kiir leadership. He has brought too much hate amongst Dinka themselves.

This time South Sudanese must force him out by any means necessary in order for South Sudan not to go through Genocide. I believe war will ensue as a result of both the recent fraudulent elections and after the referendum.

South Sudanese must now stand up in unity to change this blinded leader, the urgency is imminent, otherwise we are going to suffer forever.

Salva Kiir Mayradit Courtesy: Wikipedia

He is giving our rights away to extremists and dictators. There is a lack of food to eat, no education for our children and neither school nor hospital they can go.

This is the logo for southernsudanproject.org
Please visit the site to learn how you can help.

We Dinka Aweil, who have been marginalization under his leadership will not silent, we will not be used any longer as a weapon to increase fear in other innocent minority tribes in the South.

For too long, the Dinka have been enslaved by poverty that Salva Kiir has promised to changed. Our children allowed to be taken and sold to the North, the truths must come out. Who is the real enemy of our South Sudanese people?

Salva Kiir is trying to divide us further so that conflicts can enflame and arise and we continue to suffer. Without services we will be dependent on his government, this must stop.

We Aweil Dinka are not going to accept slavery by anyone, we refused physical slavery and economic slavery we demand our government begin to recognize our citizens and form a democracy that will benefit all.

My Aweil Brothers and Sisters and I, we call upon the Shilluk Community, the entire Equatoian Communities, and the Nuer Community to reject the ideology of both the extreme Islamists and those that beleive "they were born to rule." Salva Kiir Mayradit is a criminal, he takes advantage of his people and does not allow democracy to flourish, his lack of honor will bring war to our nation when we need peace. Peace will come with justice but not with Salva Kiir.

As President Franklin Roosevelt said "there is nothing to fear but fear itself."

William (Bol Gai) Deng is the President of Southern Sudan Project southernsudanproject.org and works many hours exposing human rights abuses, and speaking about the extreme slavery that has haunted the Aweil Dinka for decades. He believes education, hospitals and justice is the priority for his people and works continuously to help provide such. He may be contacted and reached at the following email. wiilliamdengg@yahoo.com

Chapter 7

ARAB PROJECT: SUDAN

"Oppression of Africans," Temple University African scholar Molefi Kete Asante says, "has been continuing by one Arab Sudanese leader to the next to see who can oppress African people in Sudan more than the one before. Most of these Arab leaders who pursue the *Arab project* against Africans have never condemned slavery or stopped slavery or the massacre of African Sudanese."

Ask yourself: What voices among the Arabs have you heard speaking against the enslavement of Africans? Who are the leaders of any abolitionist campaign among the Arabs? Where are any Arab Quakers or an Arabic William Lloyd Garrison or John Brown?

For nearly 130 years Islamists have pursued what Asante identifies as the *Arab Project* in Sudan to finish off the African population whether they are African traditionalists, Christian, or Muslim. Look no farther than the Darfur Genocide of 2003 where hundreds of thousands of Darfurians, *African* Muslims, were burned out of their cities, shot down in cold blood, or had to be rescued by Chad, the United Nations and the African Union. The Arab Islamists in Khartoum have been clearing the land of Africans to make room for Arab jihadists. Sudan has established itself as one of the central sites for the Syrian Arab jihadists in an effort to increase the Arab population in the country.[35]

As previously noted, the Arab League supports the Sudanese Arabs financially. The Arab League gives billions of dollars to Sudan in its anti-African campaign. This group of which the South's former enemy Sudan is a member, is the organization that South Sudan's President Kiir now wants to join?

Arab Project: Food as a Weapon of War

One of Sudan's most effective weapons of war has been in the area of food stability; starve Africans into accepting their fate as followers of Islam and imitators of Arab culture. Actor George Clooney and humanitarian John Prendergast, founders of the *Enough Project* and its investigative arm, *TheSentry.org*, charged in a *Washington Post* opinion piece that, "the government of Omar Hassan al-Bashir in Khartoum, which seized power in a coup in 1989, regularly attacked the means of food production and used starvation as a weapon against the rebellious South Sudanese populations, just as it is still doing in Darfur and the Nubia Mountains in Sudan. This resulted in localized famines and about two million South Sudanese deaths during that North-South conflict. Now that the South Sudanese have won independence, the government of Salva Kiir in Juba is using the same destructive strategies that Bashir used against them."[36]

UN sanctions monitors told the UN Security Council that "The (South Sudan) government has during much of 2017 deliberately prevented life-saving food assistance from reaching some citizens," the monitors wrote. "These actions amount to using food as a weapon of war with the intent to inflict suffering on civilians the government views as opponents to its agenda."[37]

The international group *Human Rights Watch* in its 2018 report says "the UN described South Sudan as one of the world's most dangerous places for aid workers—at least 83 killed since the conflict started in December 2013, with 16 in 2017 alone… Both sides (President Salva Kiir and former Vice President Riek Machar) obstructed delivery of aid—notably in famine affected areas of Unity and in Upper Nile—and attacked and looted humanitarian supplies and valuables in dozens of locations."[38]

In a Nov. 28, 2017 article in *Christianity Today,* Brian C. Stiller found that "South Sudan is considered, as an agronomist in Juba told us, one of the most fertile agricultural lands in all of Africa. He estimates that, if put to good use, the lands of this one nation could be the bread-basket of the continent. But as civil war wreaks its fear, people flee, and those who flee are the very ones needed to plant and harvest."[39]

With farmers unable to plant crops amidst the violence, half of all harvests have been lost, and food is scarce. An estimated 42 percent of South Sudan's population—nearly 5 million people—are suffering from severe food shortages. That number is projected to increase to 5.5 million by 2018. Famine was recently declared in part of the country, where 100,000 people are facing imminent starvation. Unless malnutrition treatment is scaled up immediately, thousands of children are likely to die.[40]

Three years of conflict and a collapsing economy in South Sudan have placed 8 million people in need of humanitarian assistance—over half of them children. At least 3.4 million people have been forced to flee their homes. And as many as 1.2 million children are out of the classroom, their educations, and futures, are in serious jeopardy.

Arab Project: Islamic Grab for Water Sources

Crops require water and the fight for water sources is growing increasingly tense. The overall question is: who will have access to the Nile River and the Great Lakes of Africa? The KDMP believes the *Arab Project* is determined to control the water sources of the Nile. South Sudan is in the middle between Ethiopia and Egypt. The surrounding Muslim countries are clearly seeking to use South Sudan as a base to monitor Ethiopia because it is a strong country that has consistently supported the interests of African people.

Talks continue in 2018 between Egypt, Ethiopia and Sudan over the dam that Ethiopia is building on the Nile River. Egypt believes the nearly five billion dollar dam will affect its share of water from the Nile while Ethiopia argues it needs more water for its people.

Meantime, Saudi Arabia has collaborated with Sudan's Arab project to build four dams, destroying the ancient African historical area of Nubia. Once built, Sudan and Saudi Arabia would like to bring two million Arabs from Arabia and Syria to populate this ancient area of Africa. In the meantime, they are displacing five million Nubians from North Sudan. Nubians are Nile River people but the Arabs are forcing them to live in the desert. However, sources of water are only half the problem.

Dangerous heavy metals used in oil production in South Sudan have leaked into drinking water used by thousands of people with life-threatening health risks. This from the German-based rights group *Sign of Hope* in a March 2016 report in *thestar.com*. Independent toxicological tests show a "direct link between the contamination of the people and the activities of the petroleum industry working in this area (northern Unity region)," said Klaus Stieglitz Hope's Vice Chairman.[41]

The situation has deteriorated much further since that 2016 report as Stieglitz updated the crisis in a new report on June 23, 2018. "The contamination of South Sudan's water can potentially condemn an estimated number of more than 600,000 South Sudanese to painful lives and early and horrible deaths," said Stieglitz, as reported by the German publication, *Deutsche Welle. Via News* reported on June 23, 2018 that, "large though this figure already is, it's likely to rise dramatically over the next years. By doing so, it might become the gravest problem facing South Sudan."[42]

In fact, because of the apparent abandonment of malfunctioning oil facilities "South Sudan's oil fields and environs are potentially littered with environmental time bombs that are leaking oil, chemicals, and other toxic materials into the environment. This, in turn, adds to the number of people killed or chronically ill. This problem has been especially well documented in Ruweng state. What also cannot be ignored is "several oil fields' proximities to the Nile, which is the main source of water for 100 million people, and which feeds into the Sudd, the vast and valuable wetlands."[43]

Reuters reports that things could get much worse as "South Sudan is planning on vastly ramping up its production of oil, which now stands at 130,000 barrels a day, to more than 300,000.[44] The petroleum sector is meant to be the source of South Sudan's future. Instead, the documents reviewed by watchdog group, *TheSentry.org* suggest oil is intimately linked to violence."

The Sentry report goes on to say that its investigation into financial documents finds transactions indicating that numerous private companies have provided support to security forces in South Sudan in the form of supplying and transporting weapons, troops, and other goods. It found a "total of 84 transactions spanning a 15-month period beginning in March 2014 and ending in June 2015" and listing "over $80 million in payments to politicians, military officials, government agencies, and private companies, many of which are directly linked to the South Sudanese government's war effort."[45]

Arab Project: Islamic Grab for Oil Resources

South Sudan's oil is a key prize that has been fought over since Chevron Corporation discovered major oil fields in South Sudan in 1978. "Khartoum's Islamic government was determined to control the oil fields from the outset, and moved to create the "Unity Province" in 1980. This creation excluded the oil regions from southern control and incorporated them into the north. The takeover of the oil districts and the introduction of sharia law in 1983 re-ignited rebellion in the south.[46]

The Kush Democratic Majority Party brought leaders in South Sudan, the US, Canada and the East African refugee camps together for a March 10, 2018 teleconference on the oil situation.

Andreya Mayom, a member of the South Sudan Oil Committee who lives in the affected region around the Ruweng oil fields, explained that Chevron Corporation began operating the oil fields around 1980. "It was not as dangerous then as today because US companies know how to take care of the environment unlike the other countries," Mayom said.

"We knew Chevron was taking care of the environment, it was clean and our animals were healthy." Mayom said things changed drastically "soon after… the rebellion started. SPLA took over the area."

Security deteriorated for oil workers and Chevron was forced to shut down oil production. Chevron reportedly sold its one-billion-dollar investment for a quarter of its value and left Sudan.*

*The Chevron Corporation, based in California, is the second largest US oil company behind Exxon Mobil.

China became involved in Sudan's southern oil fields after signing a deal with Khartoum to reopen and develop its oil industry in March 1997. Khartoum partnered with the state-owned China National Petroleum Corporation (CNPC) and a consortium of mostly Asian oil companies. CNPC obtained concessions for largely untapped oil reserves with limited competition. Other Chinese companies followed, leading to closer bilateral political and diplomatic ties.

Mayom said that by 1999 oil started up again and was exported to the world market." He added, that by 2001 "elders from Ruweng state filed lawsuits after noticing the environment and people were dying. Another lawsuit was filed by Christian Solidarity International insisting producers clean up the environment and provide compensation."

The *Crisisgroup.org* reported that "keen to tap into an underdeveloped market with, at the time, few competitors, Chinese nationals and companies flocked to South Sudan after it achieved formal independence in July 2011."[47]

Mayom said things have gotten no better under South Sudanese President Salva Kiir: "the South Sudan government is no different than the one in Khartoum. If the lives of my people are not protected, who cares who is the government? We don't need oil," Mayom says, "what we need is people protected, the environment clean for wildlife and animals for livestock. As citizens of Ruweng state, we are asking the USA, who gave us the South Sudan country today. It was a Republican administration of George W. Bush who brought peace and we need USA to put pressure on this President (Kiir) to review all the contracts they signed with Chinese and other countries and clean up the environment."

Joseph Dut echoed Mayom's words: The government is coming and taking oil and people are dying. People are benefiting from that.

We need support from the Americans and the Chinese need to shut down." Dut strongly urged fellow committee members to work to "bring in US companies. We need people to know what is going on on the ground. The pictures are real. Without those the government would deny that this is happening—but it does happen."

Dut explained that things are chaotic in South Sudan: we don't have a system in our country when it comes to legal issues... it is very corrupt. People on the ground, the people need to rise up, an uprising to bring focus... but it must be peaceful. That message needs to be sent to both China and South Sudan leaders.

Simon Tor says the South Sudan Oil Committee is doing whatever it can within South Sudan, but the people need outside help. "The Committee met with the US Ambassador in Juba talking about the oil. The Ambassador is planning to go and see the areas affected. Tor stresses that, "we need to go to the media and let them know what is going on. We need the world to know that the government is not taking care of our people."

The answer at this point, Committee members say, is outside pressure: The US has the power to do anything and we ask America to help. We want the international community to join us in forcing the South Sudanese government to listen to their people. We want American companies back in South Sudan because the American companies know how to protect the wildlife, they know how to protect the lives of the people.

The Committee members asked that those in America make the White House aware of the situation. "We ask the US administration to listen. Our voices are not being heard. We want the US government to be our voice to force the government in Juba to listen to their people in this area.

These Chinese oil companies need to be sued either in Canada or USA and we need help from American friends and Canadian friends. We need help. That is the only way we can put pressure on them and have a knowledgeable company that can handle the environment. The South Sudan Oil Committee is getting the word out—and it is not alone. A 2014 report by the Dutch NGO Cordaid found there are "strong indications that toxic waste water, drilling muds, oils spills, and chemicals have seriously polluted the environment."[48]

Chapter 8

AFRICAN VS ARAB/
ISLAM VS CHRISTIANITY:
A STARK CONTRAST

Africans need to examine the impact that Islam has had on their history and ask themselves: what are its adherents like Bashir and his minions doing to their lives? Unlike Christianity, Islam is far more than just a religion; it governs everyone's daily behavior. We know that life for indigent Africans has been one of repression and struggle for centuries and it has not improved in modern times. In fact, the formal imposition of Sharia by President Nimeiri in 1983 brought government sanctions of horrible punishments like public amputations for stealing.

Women's rights under current President Bashir are seriously restricted. They must always defer to their husbands or male guardians in managing their assets and are denied access to credit or bank loans. Females are segregated in public and must always give way to men i.e. literally go to the back of the bus. Bashir's Sharia restricts women's dress. All women, even the thousands of Christian South Sudanese refugees, must be covered from head to toe and violators can be subject to public beatings. In June 2018 a 19-year-old Sudanese woman faced a death sentence for killing her husband as he tried to rape her. Forced marriages are common and are allowed for girls as young as ten.

Religious persecution, as we learned from Pastor Tawor in chapter four, is frequently used to silence opposition. Even those who practice Islam albeit a different version, are subject to arrest or even death. Sudan's residents live in fear, critics charge, because Bashir applies Sharia at random and uses his military and militias to back it up.

South Sudan's independence in July 2011, gave Bashir's Islamic government the freedom to target its forces and resources on the rest of the African regions of Sudan like Nubian Mountains, Blue Nile, Abyei, Beja, Darfur and Nubia. These areas were sympathetic to the struggles of South Sudan. They were promised in the 2005 Comprehensive Peace Agreement the right to decide for themselves whether to officially join the country of South Sudan.

If Bashir and his cronies are successful in conquering the marginalized people of Sudan, they will then be free to focus again on South Sudan. Even now the Arab Muslims are using business and economic spies to steal as much as they can from the people of South Sudan.

Desperate to stay in power, the current South Sudan regime makes deals with the North bartering its resources in exchange. The regime has opened its arms to Chinese oil companies that have so polluted our rivers and land that babies come into the world with birth defects if they do not die in their mothers' wombs.

The Arabs' Sudanese project is so complicated it makes it difficult for any ordinary African and South Sudanese to understand what the Arabs and Islamic mission really mean. They call us "Abeds" or Abed. We call them brothers and sisters, they call us inhuman and monkeys.

As before, we shall show even more now that we are not afraid to stand up for the rights of freedom against all the enemies of the African people who are the true owners of the sacred lands. These enemies force our women into intermarriage to have more confused babies in our societies with different Arabs and Muslims names. This is a form of invasion, mental, cultural, and psychological.

No god is greater than the God of Africa. And *any* God that does not speak an *African* language is not worthy of the African people.

Sudan's Bashir on public TV contemptuously described South Sudanese as insects. Arabs ridicule the great kingdom of Kush by calling it Kushish in Arabic, which means something worthless. This is to remove us from our rich African heritage. We are the descendants of Kush. We Africans in Sudan were the first people who stood and spoke, we are the first to cross rivers, to name the days and count the moons. We called the name of God before other humans. When Muhammad created Islam in the 7th century, we had already discovered mathematics, counting, writing, agriculture and the domestication of animals.

The author of Genesis wrote, "the name of the second river is the Gihon; it winds through the entire land of Cush." (Genesis 2:13, NIV) The Sudan corresponds to the land known as Cush or Nubia, the heartland of the Nile Valley civilization. Arabs cannot lay claim to that inheritance.

Khartoum, in Dinka language means "two rivers meet and merge together" into one. This is not an Arabic word; it is African.[49] We have been badly educated, misguided, misled, misinformed and indoctrinated by Arab Muslims to deny us knowledge of ourselves, and our African identity.

Prophecy author Joel Richardson says those who study Biblical prophecy often confuse which people are involved in Ezekiel's warning in Chapter 30 that in "the day of the Lord... a sword will come against Egypt, and anguish will come upon Cush..."[50] (Ezekiel 30:3-4)

Richardson writes: "the modern day nation of Ethiopia is largely unrelated to the Ethiopia mentioned by Ezekiel. The translation of "Cush" as "Ethiopia" is actually quite misleading. Yet as a result of this widely used, but faulty translation, the poor Ethiopian people today, one of the most ancient, noble and largely Christian cultures in the earth, have gotten a seriously bad rap... the region that the

Bible refers to as Cush became known as Nubia, which the Greeks called Aithiopia. But today this region is southern Egypt and Northern Sudan."

Richardson goes on to explain that "...the ancient region of Abyssinia was much more southeast. This is where modern Ethiopia is now located. In others words, ancient Abyssinia is modern Ethiopia and ancient Aithiopia is modern day North Sudan.

"Because of this confusion," he says many students of prophecy are awaiting the Christian majority nation of Ethiopia to join with the Islamic alliance described in Ezekiel 38-39. But a correct understanding of the name Cush points us to North Sudan, not Ethiopia."

Currently Sudan is between 95-97% Muslim. Islam has controlled the national government since Sudan's independence in 1956. The remaining three percent, mostly Christian, live in the region of the Nubian Mountains where they have been targets of genocide by their own Khartoum government.

Our revolutionaries have not had historical background and have not understood Arab philosophy and religion and political ideology. Only when we see African people as the central subjects of our own history will we be able to see what has happened to us in Sudan. If we do not understand Arab racism then everything else will confuse us. The lack of information brings disinformation and when you lack information about your enemies, you are at their mercy.

The Bible teaches that "without a vision, the people perish."[51] No vision is possible without information. A strong vision of where we have come from and where we are going is crucial to bring victory in our lifetime over the enemies of Africa. That victory will not be complete without the marginalized African Sudanese from Nubian Mountains, Blue Nile, Abyei, Beja, Darfur and Nubian far North.

Chapter 9

THIS STRUGGLE IS PERSONAL: BOL GAI DENG

A Slave Child in Sudan[52]

The Dinka assign great honor to the elders of their tribe. They know their leaders' deep wisdom came from successfully leading their clan through many generations of dangerous life in the bush, negotiating seasons of floods and drought and fending off frequent attacks by invaders from other cultures. It is through this wisdom that the elders' eyes were drawn to Bol Gai Deng from the time he left the safety of his mother's womb. Witnesses say he was born with his eyes wide open "like someone who would guide his family, friends and cattle toward a good future. His cry of life like an announcement that he was present for work."

Bol Gai's father, near death when Bol was born, had a sixth sense about his newborn son's unusual strength of character. He took comfort from knowing that strength would play a large role in shaping Bol's future. He nicknamed him Bol Akonyhok (a-KON-yock) which means "he will bring home what is ours." Bol savors this story and others told by his mother and siblings because he never knew his father.

His mother kept her husband's memory alive by using his nickname for Bol. She believed the name Bol Akonyhok prophesied her son's future. She also sensed a special connection between Bol Gai and their stock. It was why she put Bol in charge of the family's cattle, their most important source of wealth, when he was just five years old. That decision was huge. Cattle are highly valued to the Dinka or Muonyjang culture. They provide milk for drinking and cooking. They pull heavy plows through the soil and their dung is used for fertilizer and fuel for cooking and heating. Cows are also used for dowries and payment of debt.

Amiir Dau Akol knew her son was bright and intelligent beyond his years. He learned quickly how to make byres for the cattle, harvest millet and rap, and move the cattle when they needed to find new pastures. It was clear to everyone that Bol would become a good leader. He had been born well and his family respected and loved him.

Bol Gai, at age seven, had already become a herder of goats and cattle. Aside from the loss of his father, Bol Gai's life was full of joy and he anticipated a happy future in his beautiful village of Cawuong. His home was not far from the rich Nile River with meadows, streams, and rainforests stretching as far as the eye could see.

One early evening, chores over, Bol was relaxed as he watched the setting sun. His mother, as always, nearby, tending to a crop of millet. He could see his brothers and sisters in the distance running back and forth in a lively game of dodgeball punctuated by frequent bursts of laughter. Fragrant smells of roasting deer filled the air. The children knew it was time to start preparing for story time when all the young would gather round and listen to the storytellers. Later, under the stars, there would be music and dancing into the night. This was a Dinka tradition and a perfect way to end a day of work in the harsh Sub-Saharan sun. It was a happy moment in time.

Subtly at first, the atmosphere of peace began to change. Livestock became restless, their unease growing louder, signaling something amiss. It was like the approach of a big storm. The earth began to reverberate with the pounding of hundreds of hoof beats, then shouts and gunfire. A raid, sponsored by government soldiers burst into the quiet and peaceful village. They began setting the huts on fire, some with people inside. Bol could hear the awful sounds of pain from his mom and his siblings as what seemed to him to be men like wild animals, coming from all directions and tearing to shreds the fabric of his home.

Clearly the peace that surrounded the villagers was to be no more. Mujahideen covered in white hooded robes on massive horses, some with masks, but all with long swords and guns, galloped through the village. They indiscriminately killed anyone who stood in their way: men and women, and some older children. The entire village was crushed like one would crush a column of ants underfoot. Cows and goats, agitated and skittish amidst the violence, were taken forcefully by the raiders. Cattle were loved and respected by the Dinka as links to the origin of the universe—anyone who did not understand that had to be worse than human.

A terrified and bewildered Bol Gai had no time to think about the loss of his favorite cow; he tried to make himself as small as he could and only hope that the raiders would tire of their destruction. But alas, this was not to be the case. Like vandals the raiders burned the village to the ground, emptied out the granaries, destroyed pottery and tools, and took many children as captives. Bol's village didn't know it then, but it was part of a series of Murahaleen raids across southern Sudan.

Frightened and separated from his family, Bol Gai began running for his life, agile and quick, like the goats he had chased after since he was four years old. For a seven-year-old, Bol proved hard to catch. Men with guns searched for him everywhere in the village and on the outskirts through thickets until they caught him. Before long, Bol Gai, whom the elders praised since his birth, found himself pulled up in front of one of the raiding horsemen, a prisoner who, along with masses of other young children, was soon forced on a long walk to the north of Sudan.

Imagine a little boy taken from his childhood village in the province of Aweil, away from his relatives, away from his own friends, and forced to walk hundreds of miles and then sold into slavery. It was a nightmare from which he thought never to awake.

Yet what happened to young Bol Gai Deng had been happening for years in Sudan. Raiders coming from the north on horses, wearing white turbans, wielding sharp knives and automatic weapons, would descend upon small unsuspecting villages and capture children as young as five years old and take them to the north to be sold into slavery to Arab traders.

Bol lost not only his freedom but his childhood. He could not do anything without the permission of the man who had "bought" him. Little Bol Gai had to get up early in the morning and tend to the goats and cattle on the farm; only this was different from the time in Aweil when he cared for the goats and cattle of his people. Here in the north among strangers he was simply carrying out the duties that were given to him by someone who claimed he "owned" him. Bol Gai could not be at leisure, doing things that he wanted to do, like playing games with other children. He could not drink or eat when he was thirsty or hungry because he had to wait until the slave owner told him he could drink or eat. His life was miserable but he came to believe that he was just as deserving as the Arab children who played when they wanted to and who ate when they were hungry.

Bol Gai always seemed to be hungry, thirsty, or sleepy. From a distance he could see other children his age playing and laughing but he was not allowed to play with them. As a slave he was also shackled with iron chains so he could not run away.

An intelligent boy, Bol Gai created ways to occupy his time. He thought a lot about his family, especially his mother and his brothers and sisters. He would recite their names, remember their cattle, and his special cow, and rejoice to himself that he was of the heroic Dinka people. When he was sad, he remembered the beauty of the Dinka cattle. They were the means of wealth and health for the Dinka. He learned to throw cow's dung long distances when he was still in his village. When no one was looking, Bol Gai would toss small pieces of the dung as far as he could, and then run out to find the piece that had been tossed the longest distance. He would put it in his pocket for luck.

Every morning that the sun came up was another day for Bol Gai to wonder when he would ever be free. He missed his family. He did not know what to do to escape from the condition he was in, so some days he would take the cattle out to feed and then tears would roll down his smooth ebony face like strings of diamonds.

One day he decided that since he was such a good keeper of cattle he would show that he was the best in the world. Using childhood training, young Bol Gai treated the cattle with so much love and respect that each one seemed to know him. As he cared for the cattle he thought how terrible it was that his "slave owner" did not treat him as he treated the cattle in his care. Was a human not as good as a cow?

Soon the owner recognized the expert care that little Bol Gai Deng was giving to the animals so he decided to take off his chains. The removal of the chains was like a small liberation. It was as if a burden and a marker as a slave had been removed from him but he knew that the removal of the chains was not true freedom because even with the removal of the chains he could not do what he pleased

Getting the cattle to water and to new grass fields became his daily challenge. One day Bol Gai lost a cow. This was considered a serious problem, a terrible fault, a horrible mistake. He was taken to a whipping post and given many lashes until his back hurt with bruises and sores bled onto his clothes. He said that he was sorry that the cow had escaped and promised that he would never let it happen again. But he knew after the whipping that the time would come when he would have to escape, that no form of slavery was good.

After having been in captivity for several years and still only about 10 years old, Bol Gai took the cattle out one beautiful morning when the sun had not yet reached the usual 100-degree plus temperature. The cattle walked the beaten path toward the grassland, leaving behind clouds of dust. They went directly to the grass and then to the water to drink. Bol Gai had a routine with each of the cows. He would prepare a paste out of cow's dung and urine, and sometimes water, and then he would wipe the paste on the horns of each cow. With this concoction no insect would dare come near the cattle.

On this beautiful day, with his work temporarily done, Bol Gai went to rest under a beautiful acacia tree, called koot (coat) in the Dinka language. It was shaped like a large umbrella with thorns. You can imagine how welcome the shade of this tree was to little Bol Gai. He dozed a bit but his brain would not stop thinking about his wonderful homeland and the village of Cawuong. In the cool of the acacia's shelter he thought of his mother asking him daily, "What can you do to become a better person tomorrow, Bol Akonyhok?" He was determined to find a way to freedom.

Just as he was thinking of freedom a train whistle blew so loud that it shocked him. It was like it was calling him. He had heard it before on other days but on this particular day, a lovely day, when he could smell the flowering bushes, and as he was resting from doing his work, dozing a little, his mother on his mind, the train's whistle sounded so good. He looked around and saw that the cattle were close to the train tracks, having wandered away as he was resting under the shade tree. He ran toward the cattle hoping to keep them from getting on the tracks where they could be killed. Many things ran through his mind, most of all what would happen to him if any of the cows were lost, maimed or killed.

Soon he could hear the screeching of the train's brakes. The engineer was so close to the cattle that Bol Gai could see his dark eyes and his beard. Soon the cattle left the tracks slowly, moving to their own rhythm and time, and Bol Gai sighed in relief.

Bol Gai could only think of how fortunate he had been that the cattle were not killed or lost. He knew the harshness and brutality of his slave owner although no one could have loved the cattle like he did. He could not hold back the words "Thank you!" Of course he said it in Dinka, "Yin aca leec," (ye EYE sha-laysh). He counted the cattle and was further relieved when he found out that not one was missing. As he guided the cows away from the train a strange thought came over his mind. What if he jumped on the train as it started to move again? Suppose he could catch a ride on the train to any place other than where he was as a slave?

The train paused as if to beckon him to ride. But how could he get on the train without the engineer seeing him? At ten years old Bol Gai had a split second to make a decision. He did not know anything about trains. He did not know where it went and he thought about how he would survive once the train stopped. He could be free or re-enslaved depending on what happened to him when the train arrived at its destination.

Like an Aweil bolt of lightning he leaped aboard the train and found a comfortable spot between the freight cars. The cattle that he had protected, rubbed down, and given food, became his saviors. They had stopped the train by wandering on the railroad tracks. He could only think of the generosity of the cattle as the huge train lumbered forth on its journey.

Bol Gai did not have much food, only the fruits that he brought with him to the pastures, and just a little water in a skin bottle. But at the first train stop he found some water and jumped back on the train between the cargo cars.

The train went through many small villages and little Bol Gai hung on for three days before it arrived in the massive city of Khartoum (kar-Toom). He had never seen so many people or a city so big. Khartoum was the capital of Sudan and Bol Gai saw many children from many different ethnic groups. He recognized those who enslaved black people and he saw people who looked like they were rich. They wore jewelry and had big cars. Everywhere he looked in Khartoum he saw people selling goods and food on the streets.

Wandering the streets as a young lost boy he was told by some other young children that he should find the refugee camp, a place where people without a place to live can get food and shelter. He found the closest refugee camp run by religious people. He was given a chance to study in a Catholic school because he loved to learn. But the government, seeing the progress of the students, decided to close the Christian schools in Khartoum.

Soldiers with guns entered the school to close it down. Once again, after seven years at the camp, Bol Gai had to run for his life. He soon found his way to Egypt, one of the oldest African countries, with the help of staff members of the school. Egypt was somewhat better than Sudan but even in Egypt because of the persecution of Africans by Arabs he was not completely safe. Bol Gai spent his days studying and waiting for relief from the oppressive situation he found himself in as a person in limbo between slavery and freedom.

Saint Bartholomew's Episcopal Church in Richmond, Virginia sponsored Bol Gai and three others which allowed them to move to the United States. Bol was so happy to hear that he would be going to this place called America. He had heard that food was available everywhere. Bol had seen a picture of the President stepping off Air Force One with his favorite dog. He decided then and there that the place where dogs were so well-fed and pampered was a place he wanted to live.

When he arrived in Virginia he received a warm welcome from the "St. Bart's" church community. Church members Frank and Jill Wood took Bol into their home where he lives to this day. Parishioner Sarah Bay spent long hours teaching him English and history to become a US citizen. Her sister Frances Boynton and many others also helped Bol tremendously along the way. In just 8 years, this initially frightened, lonely "Lost Boy" soon become an integral part of the Richmond, Virginia community, a college graduate and an active participant in political life in America.

In His Own Words: An African Slave Finds Freedom in America

My name is Bol Gai Deng. My idyllic childhood in the farming village of Cawuong in Aweil in southern Sudan was cut brutally short in 1987. Thousands of government-armed-and-funded Arab militias known as Janjaweed, so-called 'devils on horseback' galloped through our village shooting AK47s and 94s. My mother screamed "run" but I was little and couldn't keep up amid the mass panic as members of my family and our neighbors were gunned down, others stabbed to death with machetes. Some had their heads, arms and legs cut off. Bodies were thrown in neighborhood wells to poison the drinking water. The women and girls of our village were repeatedly raped.

My abductor was an Arab man about 40 years old although it was hard to be certain, as his head and body were covered in long, white robes. He saw me, pulled up his huge horse, leaned over and dragged me over his saddle. He galloped over to an open area where all the children were being grouped together. There he dropped me but I couldn't stop crying so he started beating me with a long, heavy stick. After that he left to continue attacks on other nearby villages.

We were all so scared but our nightmare had only begun. I was among hundreds of children and the next day we were forced to walk to the western part of Sudan. It felt like we walked for hundreds of miles. Our precious cows and other animals were bartered for guns and the children who could care for them were sold off with them. Others were trained to become militants.

I was sold to a wealthy landowner named Ali Abdullah who lived in the Nyala region. He owned about 50 slaves who were supervised by a militant overseer. The boss didn't care that I was only 7 years old, he forced all the children to work from morning till night.

Ali Abdullah beat me up a lot. Sometimes I slept with the cows. I had no bed, mostly I just slept out in the rain with a blanket made from a cow's hide. You scrabbled for food wherever you could find it, usually table scraps or whatever was left over from the dogs. Abdullah and his family would laugh while they ate their rich food and make fun of you. They would call you over and when you would come, they would hit you.

One young boy didn't do what the Master said so he was tied to a horse and dragged a long way. Big thick chains were tied around our legs at night so we couldn't escape. The chains would rip the skin from our ankles. We weren't schooled except for being forced to follow the Islamic religion contrary to our African beliefs and customs. I thought that my life had ended. My job was to look after the goats and cows, and it was from the long days in the pastures that I began to think of how to escape.

Finally, I saw my chance. I was out in the fields near the railroad tracks and saw a slow moving train heading to Khartoum. I jumped on board and was carried away to freedom. Wandering the streets of the biggest city I had ever seen I was befriended by two fellow Dinkas who helped me get to a refugee center. It was still hard. We were allowed to attend school but it was run by teachers who used books printed in Arabic and that was the only language we were allowed to speak.

In 1991 Osama bin Laden came onto the scene. Some claimed that he was just a wealthy businessman investing in Sudan. He was rumored to have inherited hundreds of millions of dollars. Later testimony from former lieutenants argued his business dealings hid his al Qaeda organization and the millions of resources it funneled to other international terrorist groups.[53]

Whatever the truth, the Sudanese government was beholden to bin

Laden and when he told them a year later that they should shut down Christian churches and schools the soldiers obeyed. Students were told to stay at the schools. Soldiers began going through the school buildings taking them into custody. I knew it was time to leave. After harrowing fits and starts I finally made it from the refugee camp in Khartoum to more squalid conditions in Egypt.

I finally found people who could help me. They were from the United Nations and many of us found ourselves standing in line for appointments praying to get accepted to move to the West. We heard lots of rumors and warnings about the interviewers. We must not get a certain female officer; she was tough as nails, we were told, and rarely approved anyone's application. As luck would have it, I drew this woman. I couldn't sleep the night before; all I could do was pray she would treat me kindly. She lived up to her reputation and I sweated through some extremely tough questions. Finally, miracle of miracles, she approved my application! Soon I was on my way to the United States.

In America I found a freedom I never knew in either Sudan or Egypt. I could travel where I wanted, eat what I wanted, and listen to any speech or make any speech I wanted. When I first arrived in Virginia, I worked a few menial jobs, but soon realized I wanted more out of life. I applied and was accepted to J. Sargent Reynolds Community College. After attending that school for one year, I transferred to the larger Virginia Commonwealth University. I felt very comfortable here. There were lots of immigrants from everywhere. I started fitting in more and looking to my future. VCU officials took me under their wing and helped me register for the right classes and I was on my way.

Then came 9/11. America was under attack by the same Islamic extremists who had invaded my homeland and savaged my people. I was outraged and became deathly afraid for the future of my adopted country. I wanted to give back for all America had given to me. I spoke fluent Arabic and I thought it was something I could use to help America so I signed up for Homeland Security.

I found other ways to help America, other Sudanese refugees and those back home. I founded the Southern Sudan Project (SSP) and helped co-found the Aweil Youth Association of the United States, serving as its president in 2011. I am the first of my family to read and write. Our culture was not about education, it was about farming and herding cattle. Tragedy to my community brought me to America and I learned that education is very important. I set up the Dinka Fellowship Church at St. Bartholomew's Church in Richmond's West End. Members of the Sudanese community meet evenings to worship and share experiences.

I found that the lack of education was hindering my fellow refugees, especially the women. I believe that if you teach the women, you teach the kids. I went to VCU and asked for help for the immigrant mothers who didn't speak English or have life skills to be successful here. They gave me a room on campus and we opened classes in English. Total Access Preparatory Academy, or TAPA, was born.

We are finding that as our mothers learn to speak English and life skills they discover a sense of self-esteem that has spread to the entire family and brought them closer together. What started as one class to teach Sudanese women English soon expanded to men and children not only from Sudan but refugees from all over the world.

Most TAPA students graduate knowing how to read, write, text, Skype, and use a video camera. They use I-phones and computers, go online and find Sudanese communities in Denmark, Canada, Australia, the refugee camps in East Africa and Sudan. I have been so impressed by what education can do. These refugee women are taking better care of their children and themselves.

After the 2005 Comprehensive Peace Agreement was signed I saved money and was finally able to go home and see the fate of my family. Many of my brothers and sisters were dead. I found remaining neighbors the same as when I left after the attack, lost. Seeing them scarred by such violence and brutality, I became determined to help my people develop a vision of what they can do and how far they can go. The Islamic government in Khartoum didn't give women access to education and even a lot of men in Sudan didn't know how to read and write. The literacy rate today is about 27% in South Sudan.

My goal is to take the TAPA education model and establish classes in South Sudan and then the marginalized areas, among them Darfur, Nubian Mountains, Blue Nile, and Abyei. The marginalized people, Muslim and Christian, were all part of the 2005 Peace Agreement. They were to have a vote on staying with Sudan or going with South Sudan. The month after South Sudan voted for independence July 9, 2011, Khartoum soldiers invaded the Abyei region, killing two thousand women and children and displacing thousands of others who fled to South Sudan.

Despite his promises in the peace agreement, Sudan's President Bashir continues his ethnic cleansing campaign against the African people and culture. He has not released all the South Sudanese enslaved by Arab masters and African slave trafficking continues today. Bashir is wanted by the International Criminal Court for war crimes against humanity.

Meantime, in South Sudan, the happiness and celebration of our independence has long since faded. Our infrastructure is virtually non-existent from decades of war. We are the richest country in Africa in terms of resources but our leaders are inexperienced. Once the 2005 CPA was signed the army disintegrated into rival factions and fighting. There has been looting of billions of dollars and huge corruption.

The North is not sitting back watching. North Arab traders are coming in and doing business and taking profits to the North. To maintain power, President Kiir has signed agreements with largely Chinese oil companies who have devastated our environment. There is disease and babies are born with major deformities. There are reports of Russian special forces on the scene as these outsiders seek to get control of our land and resources. We have just traded one dictatorship for another and potentially good leaders are afraid to stand up for fear of reprisal. I receive regular reports of brutal intimidation by government security forces on anyone who opposes the current regime.

After everything that I have lived through, I learned that South Sudanese lived in our own little world. When I first came to America it was about me, how to live and become rich. I soon learned that the United States of America, means just that, *united*. While everyone has differences when there is a crisis or need in the community, everyone comes together. It is about humanity, the "government by the people, for the people." I now know that as an American citizen it is not about me, it is about tomorrow and the next generation.

We have to bring that vision to the people of South Sudan. Our country suffers from a lack of identity, a national identity. We have ethnic identities, even religious identities, but we need national pride. This will help us overcome our ethnic and religious differences. The women care more about vision than the men. They care about the innocents and the need for an identity, a vision, for the entire community. The vision has to be fully expanded to the male population as well.

Preparing to Lead

Bol Gai Deng's journey has been one of oppression, subjugation, rebirth, struggle, and victory over those who sought domination. His early life became a succession of miracles that saw him overcome enormous odds, culminating in a new life in the United States. There he also beat grim statistics that would normally predict failure; persevering to learn English at night while working menial jobs by day, winning acceptance to college, and earning degrees in Political Science and Homeland Security at Virginia Commonwealth University. His choice of study was no accident. It was carefully considered in light of his growing desire and constant prayer to help his people in South Sudan and, after 9/11/2001, in America, his adopted country.

Bol's leadership skills were immediately apparent with life-changing results for those who took advantage of the opportunities he created. He wasted no time putting his studies to work organizing Sudanese refugees in America, Canada and abroad, resulting in the *Aweil Youth Association, USA (AYA)*, to unite the children of Sudan, many of whom were enslaved; to promote democracy and human rights in Sudan; the *Southern Sudan Project (SSP)*, a US-registered, 501(c)(3) non-profit organization to build schools in South Sudan, along with *TAPA* which helped Sudanese and other African women learn English, math and computer skills to equip them for better paying jobs in the United States. Dozens of students from nine countries have been through the classes preparing them to test for a GED and assisting in their pursuit to obtain American citizenship.

Bol believes that women are key in forging a new future for South Sudan and Africa as a whole. Providing women access to education will put them in a better position to provide an education for their children. TAPA's mission also focuses on women's leadership roles. Ninety percent of women in Sudan cannot read or write; rape is an ongoing fear and Sudan has the highest rate of maternal deaths in the world. The struggles of Sudanese women have largely been ignored. Bol strongly believes that it is the women who could lead the way to peace in Sudan. They need their human rights restored and a safe place where they can flourish and find their own "voice."

It wasn't long before Virginia made note of Bol's achievements both at school and in the community. In 2008 he was presented with the *Black History in the Making* Award from VCU's Department of African American Studies.

Bol Enters America's Political Arena
on behalf of South Sudan

Sudan's unfair elections in the summer of 2010 resulted in sustained fighting and the arrest and exile of several independent political candidates. Bol worked with US Representatives to initiate a meeting between those candidates and the Foreign Relations Committee. He could also be found at rallies at the White House in Washington and the United Nations in New York.

The rise in prominence of General Salva Kiir after Dr. John Garang's death in 2005 was also on Bol's radar. His concern over Kiir's motives prompted a warning via an opinion piece published in the July 15, 2010 edition of the Salem News.[54]

Bol's fears have been confirmed many times over. Then, as now, those in a position to change the trajectory of South Sudan's future, the world community through the United Nations and the United States, did not listen. Millions of people have died, suffered the horrors of intimidation through gang rapes and other violence, and millions in South Sudan are on the brink of starvation.

Bol continued his outreach, protesting what was happening in South Sudan and Sudan. He also continued organizing both inside the country and out, preparing for the day when powerful people would wake up and force Sudan and South Sudan's corrupt leaders off the world stage.

Bol was named Associate Professor of Homeland Security at VCU for the school year 2011-2012. Also in 2011 Bol was elected and served as CEO/President of the Aweil Youth Association US and served until 2015.

In 2012 Bol founded *African Kauda*, a nation-wide group that prayed to overturn South Sudan President Salva Kiir's secret sale of Aweil land (known as 14 mile) to the Khartoum regime. When the story broke in the media, Aweil leaders tried to claim the land. African Kauda met regularly to pray for Aweil's success.

Bol and his team organized a coalition of human rights groups, including the *Marginalized People of Sudan* and rallied at the United Nations, protesting the criminal actions of President Bashir's Khartoum regime. Out of that protest came a "think tank" on the subject of Sudan genocides at the Desmond Tutu Center in NYC on November 25, 2011, which was attended by representatives from Blue Nile, Darfur, Nubian Mountains, Abyei, Beja, and Nubia in Sudan.

Bol foresaw the importance of political skills in preparing for the future. *SSP*, in conjunction with the non-profit *American Epiphany*,[55] held a "Fieldman's School" in 2012 in Richmond to teach political campaign organization to Sudanese activists from across the United States and Canada. The skills they learned in this school allowed Kush Democratic Majority Party team leaders to prevail in hotly contested races for leadership of AYA US and Aweil Community Association US from 2015-2017.

South Sudan President Salva Kiir, realizing the growing popularity of the Kush Democratic Majority Party, had sent large sums of money and people to oppose KDMP's candidates at the two organization's conventions. Bol credits the skills his people learned at the Richmond Fieldman School as instrumental in KDMP retaining leadership of both conventions.

Bol spent countless hours networking and fundraising on behalf of the oppressed people of Sudan. He went to Uganda to coordinate and deliver with Dr. Al Sutton and the *Nuba Mountains International Association* $800,000 of medical supplies to Sudanese refugee camps. He also helped in delivery of another million-dollars-worth of medical

95

supplies. In a second trip to Sudanese refugees, they supplied 35,000 meals of therapeutic food.

As the government of South Sudan President Salva Kiir and his bitter war with his former Vice President Riek Machar became more deadly and Kiir's persecution of opponents grew in intensity, it became clear that South Sudan needed major change. Bol Gai Deng, child of Aweil with an African hero's blood in his veins, a former slave, escapee, Egyptian refugee and finally, college-educated citizen of the United States was nominated as Kush Democratic Majority Party's candidate for President of South Sudan. He kicked off the campaign in April 2017. His team's Trump-like use of social media is spreading their message across the world.

Nubian Mountains humanitarian activist Nazar Suliman heard KDMP's message. He deeply believes Bol is the only leader on the horizon who is capable of building a humanitarian-based government. South Sudan and Sudan have never had such a possibility, the people have always been at the mercy of warlords who only understand leadership by violence. Suliman is confident that Bol's election victory would soon allow his own Nubian people to vote on whether to join South Sudan as promised in the Comprehensive Peace Agreement. Frustrated by the taunts of pro-regime workers, Suliman posted questions on Facebook to answer KDMP's critics and encourage others who are reluctant to air grievances against the current regime out of fear of reprisal:

"Let me say this, it's ok to support your boss (President Salva Kiir). It's called democracy. It's not ok to criticize someone else for stepping up or claim that everything is fine in South Sudan when it is not. Research answers to the questions below to learn why Bol Gai decided to give up his beautiful life in the USA to help rescue his people and his country:

1. When was President Salva Kiir's term supposed to end?

2. Where has all the money from South Sudan's oil gone?

3. Why has President Kiir "voluntarily" asked to join the Muslim Arab League (the same Arab people who slaughtered more than 5 million South Sudanese people—the first, longest and deadliest jihad war in the world)?

4. Why are nearly half of the South Sudanese people still refugees, and live in refugees camps in neighboring countries, while South Sudan has enough resources to feed everyone?

5. Why are foreign Muslim organizations controlling private schools and businesses in South Sudan—what are their intentions?

6. Who benefits from illegal militias and unlawful soldiers?

7. Why is it illegal for South Sudanese to run for President?

8. How many people have died under Salva Kiir's regime? Who is responsible and why has no one been brought to justice?

9. Why is President Kiir not scheduling elections?

10. Who is behind all the chaos and violence to prevent the scheduled elections in 2018?

11. Why is President Kiir afraid of Bol Gai Deng?

Suliman focuses on a major sticking point: the world community's reluctance to demand free, fair elections in 2018 as promised in the Comprehensive Peace Agreement. South Sudan's regime knows that violence is keeping elections at bay and the regime in power. KDMP's efforts to this point had been focusing on pressuring the United Nations and the US State Department, Members of Congress, Sudanese groups and representatives from refugee camps in East Africa to stick to the 2018 election time frame.[56]

Bol and his KDMP team leaders are aware of the gibes posted on social media platforms and the lack of support in some quarters that is given credence by news reporters, but they understand all too well the fear and rivalry that prompt them. They know detractors and fear of Kiir discourage other potential supporters from speaking out. Bol reminds the frightened that the prophet Nehemiah faced similar obstructions in his mission to rebuild the wall protecting the city of Jerusalem. Just like the KDMP, Nehemiah had to deal with "a land that had been inhabited by so many people that there were mixed feelings in regard to the Hebrews reinhabiting the land." While most supported Nehemiah, there were "two characters named Sanballat and Tobiah" [who]"were threatened…who feared they would lose their power over the people. So their first strategy was intimidation and verbal abuse. Nehemiah prayed. Then they tried to discourage the workers. Nehemiah reminded them of God's help. Then they sank to a new level of threats of physical abuse. Nehemiah…set up battle strategies with them. Finally, Sanballat and Tobiah threatened to assassinate Nehemiah. Nehemiah prayed again but he didn't back down…those builders finished the wall in less than two months… and marched on top of it around the city to celebrate."[57]

Bol personally, his family as symbolized by his grandfather's legacy, and the persecuted thousands of KDMP supporters around the world have faced their fears and experienced miracles over and over again. They know that faith and prayer will conquer fear and that they will also celebrate the victory of their God-inspired mission.

Chapter 10

KUSH DEMOCRATIC MAJORITY PARTY

Our fellow citizens in South Sudan and marginalized areas of Sudan are under unprecedented economic, political and institutional oppression from centuries-old enemies of the African people. Thus the Kush Majority Party is ready to engage in all ways necessary to restore African greatness.

Following are issues that we must confront:

Collapse of democratic, political and economic institutions of governance, and the corruption of our democracy by those who would acquiesce to the dictates of those who have never had our best intentions in their minds. This means that we must built institutions capable of handling a true democracy.

Who would have thought that the heroic people of South Sudan would now be confronting the specter of becoming victims of our own success? How could it be that the people of John Garang find themselves fooled and tricked by those who would rob Africa of its victory?

After so many decades of war and the victory handed to us by our dead heroes we now find ourselves seeking assistance from outside. We are capable of making the sacrifices necessary to bring a new reality.

South Sudan, beautiful South Sudan, a country once thought of as rich and powerful because of its courage and history has been turned into a country where our enemies have revised the political and intellectual history of the nation. We can and must have political pluralism, a free press, an active and dynamic civil society, a vibrant intelligentsia, a Pan-African commitment, a loyal army, and peaceful, civil response among losers and winners post-elections.

Based on our analysis of our country's present situation, we believe South Sudan's biggest stumbling block is lack of unity among indigenous Africans. We have launched the Kush Democratic Majority Party to unite all of our people no matter their faith or station in life. Our campaign is also inspired by the great development of our times: the "Consciousness Movement:" the critical 150-year-old struggle of Africans on the continent and in the Diaspora for Pan-Africanism, the political union of all the indigenous inhabitants of Africa.

We declare ourselves to be citizens conscious of our historical responsibilities who refuse forevermore to surrender the power to decide the affairs of our community to those not willing to join the Consciousness Movement.

Further, we are citizens fully aware that South Sudan needs a major, unprecedented citizen-driven end to politics as usual. We know that everything about politics is not bad since politics, in the sense of serving and not helping oneself, is fundamentally a noble enterprise.

Further, we are citizens possessed of a strong will to be, first and foremost, beyond the necessary critique, a constructive force, a builder of the present and the future, and not to be a dweller of the past. If the past belongs to the past, let the present and the future be ours!

We are fundamentally a citizen political movement that believes deeply in the renewal carried by female leadership. Gender equality and treatment, policies that enable women's greater autonomy, and policies that systematically promote women's role and place in South Sudan's political, economic, cultural and social rebirth, will be central in all areas of South Sudanese life. This separates us from others who choose to keep women back. For us, the liberation and freedom of women is not an act of charity but a necessary part of our revolution!

Our defining political identity is furthermore our deep conviction that only a true grassroots citizen discussion, with a wide, democratic, popular, non-elitist scope, in our national languages, in the most remote as well as in the buildings in the major cities, could allow South Sudan to experience a true democratic renaissance, which will allow us once for all, like all great democracies, to prevent any possibility of dictatorial drift or to marginalize counter-power mechanisms (the press, civil society, education).

The Kush Democratic Majority aims to achieve in South Sudan a genuine separation and real balance of power, in sum, a strong system of "Checks and Balances" to stop state abuses in Africa is not, in our eyes, a question of regime type: parliamentary or presidential! Africa knows presidential as well as parliamentary regimes that are now work against their people. For us, the true institutional revolution consists first in giving the power inherited from former colonial masters to the citizens, fully recognized as the only legitimate source of democratic and republican power.

Our country and our people want a true national reconciliation:

True reconciliation of the political class, through a consensual electoral code, immediate and sincere abandonment of incessant manipulations of the Constitution, a return to democratic civility and republican elegance, the end of the manipulation of the religious sector for political and electoral purposes, the public must be a neutral, strong and respected administration, the quest for the equality of all citizens, all religious denominations, and all ethnic communities before the law, and the continuing reassertion of our nation's non-religious and republican foundation.

Armed with this vision, the KDMP proposes ten priorities:

1. Restore the rule of law and its fundamental institutions, promote constitutional patriotism and the priesthood of public service for a virtuous Republic, while at the same time placing citizens at the beginning and end of our political and institutional system; and, in this context, give the Administration back to Administration professionals, and put an end to the all-out transformation of administrative bodies into political strongholds;

2. Create a new opening for the management of public affairs and the governance of private enterprises, and aggressively combat corruption and poor governance, by instituting laws that cannot be manipulated;

3. Encourage the organization of a healthier and more credible political game, with a limited number of political parties next to a strong citizen movement and an omnipresent civil society involved in the monitoring and control of the political system, while reintroducing ethics in political life;

4. Revitalize our economy through a transparent management of the country's resources, fiscal discipline and budgetary rigor, a sense of priorities for public expenses, a true poverty eradication strategy, and an exemplary and transparent cooperation with development partners and international financial institutions;

5. Launch a true program of rural development and regional development, as well as promote and valorize all aspects of our agriculture and livestock while preserving our environment and culture, through a rigorous management of our natural resources;

6. Rehabilitate, expand, and revitalize the industrial base, and strengthen the fishing industry as a key sector in our country, while giving a new impetus to other priority sectors, such as infrastructures, education, health, energy, mining, and environment;

7. Position South Sudan as one of the first countries in the world for the promotion of women and gender, for the respect and protection of human rights, freedom of the press, and civil society actions, in concert with cultural policies geared toward the youth. In order to achieve this, our country must develop a true women promotion policy, a true cultural policy, a true promotion of the press and civil society actors, and a true policy for the youth, the goal being to give our country a solid cultural, artistic, and sports community;

8. Build a real bridge with the immense resources represented by the South Sudan Diaspora everywhere in the world; a Diaspora which is not conceived as a « cash cow » to make up for a faltering State, but as quality human resource, enjoying respect, value, and invited to take a full part in an emerging and democratic South Sudan;

9. Confirm the nation's status through the consolidation of the four strong axes, that is, peace diplomacy, mediation and good neighborhood, economic and development diplomacy, Pan-African and political and economic unity of the continent, sovereignty diplomacy, alongside a valorization of diplomatic work and a restoration of the dignity associated with a diplomatic career;

10. Reaffirm our country's leadership in the Pan-African struggle in the spirit of John Garang, through a reiteration, as part of the oath taken by any new President, of a total adherence to the sacred objective of the realization of the United States of Africa, even making it a constitutional clause for our nation.

All South Sudanese must make this Manifesto a point of discussion and discourse about our future. The people must take their government and make it the progressive government it was intended to be by the patriots who gave their lives fighting for us. KDM calls the people together to provide safety, security, and peace for all the citizens of our state. In this drive for unity we cannot fail!

To this end, let us create without delay, throughout the national territory and within the entire *SOUTH SUDAN THIS POWERFUL NEW VISION FOR DIGNITY AND RESPECT!*

Our first and most urgent act will be a sustained national and international campaign against any attempt to suppress presidential election run-offs. Not only does such an attempt reveal its defenders' real electoral and existential anxiety, but it also represents a major attack on our Constitution already in tatters, and it could deal a fatal blow to our country's democratic gains.

LONG LIVE THE KUSH DEMOCRATIC MAJORITY!

JUBA, JUNE 2014[58]

Chapter 11

THE KUSH DEMOCRATIC PARTY ON THE MOVE

On April 7, 2017 ahead of the elections scheduled for 2018 as pledged in the Comprehensive Peace Agreement, Bol Gai Deng announced he was a candidate for President of South Sudan under the Kush Democratic Majority Party banner. His announcement, like so much of the KDMP's campaign, was posted on Facebook and shared around the world:

> When the sovereign state of South Sudan proclaimed its freedom from Sudan in 2011, there was hope among the people that they could have a democracy and freedom from Islamic terrorism at last. But South Sudan needed the support of the American government to survive, and the Obama administration did not seem sympathetic. And so in 2013, the country was hit hard by a war between the supporters of President Salva Kiir Mayardit and those of Dr. Riek Machar Teny. At the same time, the economic climate deteriorated day by day. Many people died from starvation, disease, and the war, while the politicians benefited from South Sudan's resources, including oil reserves. The citizens suffered greatly and are still suffering today. Millions left South Sudan seeking protection from foreign countries; many even went back to Sudan, despite human rights violations and Arab racism against Africans.

> It's time to end these atrocities. Our fundamental goal is to restore peace, bring unity, and prosperity to the people, which include the introduction of agriculture, education and development of infrastructures. A democracy is what the people need in South Sudan, but with the current South Sudanese administration, democracy seems dead. There shall be a rule of law that guides the nation from corrupt officials and radical Islamic terrorism. While dictatorship had been a part of the history in Islamic Sudan, with the new nation of South Sudan, we must now intervene and make the change for democracy for the people.

> That's why I am declaring my candidacy for the President of

South Sudan in 2018, to restore prosperity and freedom in our country and to make South Sudan a strong ally to the United States of America in Africa.[59]

From then on it has been a whirlwind of teleconferences with KDMP team leaders worldwide, live interviews on the Facebook website, other internet outlets, radio, and newspaper. Bol and his team spent many days and long hours meeting with officials at the United Nations in New York, American diplomats and Members of Congress in Washington and South Sudanese refugees all over the land. US President Donald Trump had just been inaugurated four months earlier after his extremely successful campaign heavily dependent on social media and his famous "tweets" on the Twitter sharing website. His "under the radar" effort shocked virtually every political and media expert and resulted in an unprecedented, unexpected victory in the US November 2016 elections. The KDMP decided to adopt Trump's winning strategy.

It has been a time of extreme patience and faith. The world community's confusion about the fundamental issues in South Sudan and throughout Africa causes many missteps in international peace-making efforts. Meantime, lack of money, media engaged on numerous other causes, and fear of reprisal from President Kiir's regime back home and in the East African refugee camps makes each tiny step forward a major victory. Every meeting or letter to American and United Nations diplomats brings KDMP closer to its goal of free, fair elections in South Sudan.

Despite continuing intimidation efforts and threats from the Kiir regime and its supporters, Bol keeps up the pressure as shown on this post August 25, 2017:

> "I am here to remind South Sudanese youth, women, and children: Kiir Mayardit, Riek Machar are not fighting for you, they are killing our children so their family members can take your wealth and live abroad. Enough is Enough I am asking both of them to face

Bol Gai Deng in 2018 election. They must put their guns down. Let's fight over a war of ideas to build a brighter future for South Sudan."

September 11th is a "day of infamy" not only for Americans but newly arrived South Sudanese refugee Bol Gai Deng who watched the New York towers fall and remembered Osama bin Laden's personal threat to his life several years earlier in Khartoum. He told himself that bin Laden drove him out of his home country and now he was coming after America. "No way," Bol Gai Deng vowed. He would fight bin Laden and Islamic jihad with everything he had. He offered his knowledge of Islam and fluency in Arabic to America's premier law enforcement agencies. It was too early in 2001 but by the time Bol graduated from VCU American security agencies asked to take him up on his offer. At that point Bol had become increasingly anxious about the deteriorating situation in Sudan and thought it best to continue organizing and training the South Sudanese communities. Every September 11th Bol renews his vow to defeat Islamic terror but believes that the ballot box, not guns are the way as he noted on this September 11, 2017 FB post:

> Elections are the only way we can bring peace and unity in South Sudan so Salva Kiir and Riek Machar will step aside. The majority of South Sudanese are becoming aware that these two men are driven by their greed and selfishness. We will not allow anyone to decide what is best for us as South Sudanese, because we knew what's best for us. We are asking the United States, international community, African Union and IGAD to get ready to oversee free, fair elections in South Sudan in 2018.

Bol's message resounds with all who hear it. Thousands watch his live and re-broadcasts of internet interviews. They may not have electricity in their homes, but most younger South Sudanese have cell phones. When word comes that Bol will be interviewed, supporters walk miles to reach a generator to recharge their phone batteries. One phone carrying Bol's message reaches an average of 40 people, so thousands are exposed to KDMP's vision. However, showing public support in South Sudan for the KDMP campaign means making yourself a target for Kiir's internal security forces. "We need to see you here," they plead over and over, "when are you coming? How can we believe you are not just a FB candidate if you don't come to Africa?"

The three fronts of KDMP's campaign, i.e. unifying the South Sudanese to realize their rights to human dignity and freedom; pressuring the international community to push for elections; and pressuring the Kiir regime and his rival Riek Machar to step aside; were vying for the same resources, most notably, the candidate's time and money. Believing that he was doing all that could be done to lobby world leaders and knowing that solidifying the trust of his people was growing increasingly urgent, Bol knew it was time to head to Africa.

East Africa: May 2018

The Kush Democratic Majority Party's social media campaign is effective in spreading hope among the people in South Sudan and refugees in the East African camps, United States, Australia and Europe. We learned just how effective when Bol made a May 2018 trip to East Africa. Bol's KDMP team spent 9 days there beginning with Ethiopia, Uganda, and then Kenya. He met with Kush Democratic Majority Party leaders from the refugee camps in all three countries as well as from South Sudan, South Sudanese student group leaders from universities across the region, and heads of churches both from South Sudan and the marginalized areas of Sudan. The team also spent time with countless refugees who came, on their own, to tell Bol of their struggles and desperate desire to return home to resume their lives and live in peace. Many walked long miles to share their concerns and had not eaten in days.

There was one young mother from Juba, carrying her baby, who was disowned by her family after her husband was arrested for humanitarian protests against Salva Kiir's government. She had not eaten in three days and a KDMP security team member found her sitting on the ground with her baby outside our hotel. She told him that she had heard the new President was coming there and she just wanted to see him. Bol and his supporters gave her food, some money and talked with her about her husband and her fears about the future.

The violence and persecution of the people in South Sudan have been unrelenting. The world mistakenly calls it a civil war between tribes. In reality it is a fight for power between current President Salva Kiir and his former Vice President Riek Machar. The people of South Sudan have been caught in the middle. Add to that outsiders like Russia, China and the Islamic North who want South Sudan's oil, gold, uranium, land and other resources. The result is that millions have died in the violence while six million are on the brink of starvation. Food is being used as a weapon of war and anyone who even appears to oppose Kiir's rule, even members of his own military, is either killed or placed under house arrest. Four million people have become refugees.

With all the chaos, the world community will not call for elections. They say until there is peace there can be no elections. Bol and KDMP have lobbied the UN and the US government explaining the folly of that for it is this chaos that keeps Kiir in power. The UN placed its faith in the eight East African countries that make up the International Governmental Authority for Development (IGAD) to negotiate the peace in South Sudan. The idea was ludicrous because each of those countries has a vested interest in the outcome. IGAD's efforts ended in repeated failure.

At that point, Sudan's Bashir, our former tormentor and most feared ruler in Africa, stepped up. He, with long-time Kiir ally Ugandan President Yoweri Museveni, negotiated a ceasefire and brokered a peace agreement between Kiir and Machar. Bashir is the very dictator who continues to perpetrate the persecution and genocide of Christians in the South and the marginalized people in the North. He has been wanted since 2009 by the International Criminal Court for those very crimes against our people! Bashir and Museveni, with the corrupt South Sudanese leaders Kiir and Machar are brokering a selfish deal dividing power and resources for themselves—not to help the desperate people of South Sudan.

It would be laughable if it were not so tragic. Bol pleads with the world community to intervene and prevent this farce—this spear through the heart of the South Sudanese people. It is unacceptable and cannot be borne. "It is beyond cruel to force us to succumb to our tormentors—I still carry the scars from the chains with which Bashir's minions enslaved me at age seven," Bol says.

The people of South Sudan are very clear on what they want: a humanitarian leader who believes in a country of just laws, equally applied, with power in the hands of the people. Women, victims of brutal rape, want to be protected and allowed to fulfill their own potential. During the KDMP's May East African trip, leaders of all the various groups gave Bol results of polls of their communities—90% want Salva Kiir to step down. They call Bol continually, they write and message him on social media, begging him to come and take over, even by military means if necessary. Bol knows more violence is not the answer. The answer has to be Salva Kiir stepping down and free, fair elections.

Bol was especially interested in talking with South Sudanese women from universities in Kenya, Uganda, Ethiopia and South Sudan—women who hold not only college degrees, but *masters* degrees. They told of going home and applying for jobs. Would-be employers just tossed their degrees aside saying "I don't care about this, I am only interested in your going to bed with me."

Bol was also deluged with many letters from South Sudanese refugees. Here are snippets from a few of them:

From a member of our Uganda team:

> You're brave and so worthy... I promise to stand behind you to the end, the Yirol people where I come from are known for speaking once and sticking to their words. We'll continue together in the midst of struggles until success finds us, there's nothing to worry about, chief. I am glad to have known you, the future president of the Republic of south Sudan. Let's unite and make it together, comrade. Keep the spirit, we're on your back. God bless you.

Daniel Deng Kueth Madhan:

> Turning 20 years old this December. Am a man who believe in myself that I can make somethin good for my people and country.

We once form a Secondary schools league under SPLM last year... I was appointed to be the information secretary. And our chairman was really happy for my work. Just wanna let you guys help me understand how politics is though am this young. I believe that future is us. I want the best for this country and its people. I believe yu Kush can make it coz you r all youths who are educated. Who know the meaning of life and it's importance. Thanks a lot to Amel for making me reveal... the feeling I've been hiding inside me."

Jacob Kout in Egypt:

Great move Chairman, keep up your visit around the world. It will be better then those whom were carrying the guns to kill innocent people. We are behind you. God is great our future president. God selected you, please never give up. you are popular. The way you begin is very interesting. Look forward, we are behind you. Let them talk, the God knows.

Athieng Garang from Kenya:

Great thanks to you Sir, your visit to East Africa... Make positive life to many south Sudanese who are here in kenya. Many sent me (FB) friends request. Some call me and write to me and I talk with many on the street of Nairobi. They wanted to know more... I'm ready to tell them all the things you told me during our three days together. I can now tell you Kush party will challenge all the SPLM and other parties in South Sudan at all levels from local government to National government. People are ready to be MPs, state governors on Kush ticket. God bless for making it reality.

Dhieu Ariik from Uganda:

Thank God for taking you back safely. But before that congratulations upon winning the trust of S. Sudanese in East Africa and beyond . We always seeing the media dominated by your campaigns.

Angok of South Sudan in Uganda:

Greetings my president, I pray and hope that you're well there?

First and foremost, I would like to register my appreciation to God Almighty for tirelessly standing with you in your continental trip, especially across East Africa… bringing and returning you back safely to US in the midst of ruthless and diabolic men (the so called unknown gunmen) of South Sudan. It was great protection and for that, we give thanks to God Almighty for the great job.

On a similar breath, I would like to register my sincere and heart-felt appreciations to yourself in particular for the great mission you embarked on fearlessly and also, for giving all the South Sudanese youth an opportunity to meet and share their views with you openly… great hospitality, responsibility, concern and determination in you to change the lives of young men in the Sudan for the good of their livelihoods in generations to come.

Personally, I must say, I was very honored and privileged to have met you in person. It was a great pleasure to have met and shared views with you despite being short lived. But I believe another great opportunity will come and we shall even do much bigger things together than this. You're great, brave and focused, I salute you, comrade. Your trip has been wonderful, I must admit and that's generated you and our party massive support by the masses from all walks of life. I want to tell you that your trip has changed many things and many of the masses you have met on the grassroots are far hoping for a change they will see, fell and benefit on, not just words. Many have already know that there's a party called KDM who's ready to bring the unprecedented sufferings of our people to an end. We're only being held back by fear but honestly, everywhere lives our supporters and all these was brought forth by your trip.

We're beating the odds and we can surprise the world. It's a matter of belief and determination, comrade. We can do it.

The starving, terrorized people who met Bol and the KDMP team only wanted to have someone listen to their concerns. They were in danger being there, as was Bol, Nazar and the team. Angok mentioned "ruthless and diabolical men." The team says they were there from the time we left the airport in Ethiopia headed for Uganda. Two security men from South Sudan were on the plane with us, even after we changed flights to avoid them.

In Uganda, hotel staff alerted Nazar that the Director of South Sudan's National Security Agency, General Akol Koor (who is also President Salva Kiir's brother-in-law) had arrived at our hotel with several of his men, and had leased the entire floor above our rooms. They followed us from location to location and while Nazar and our security team had closed off entry to unauthorized people, they would stand across the street from the entrance, racking their guns, trying to intimidate my people. General Koor himself went to the manager of one hotel where an event was planned and ordered him to shut it down. When he refused, Koor then went to the police chief who came and ordered the event cancelled.

Bol Gai says Salva Kiir knows his days as President are numbered. General Koor claimed to Ugandan officials that I and the KDMP were trying to destroy South Sudan, but in fact it is President Kiir who has squandered every chance he's been given to end the violence and bring peace. It is he, through General Koor and his forces, who have killed opponents while Kiir's regime has looted the treasury.* There is only one answer: Kiir must resign NOW. Then the people must be allowed their say in who leads their country.

"The East African trip has humbled and inspired me," Bol admits, "I knew we had a lot of support, but we are overwhelmed with the reception we received." Bol believes that KDMP needs to continue moving forward and pressing our case. We need to increase awareness that South Sudan is on the brink of major, positive change which will affect the future of all of Africa.

As we continue to raise awareness and push for Kiir to resign, I am reaching out to the most successful free enterprise and democratic systems in the world. Among them: the United States and Israel. Experts with proven track records will help us shape plans for a

*See the Sentry.org discussion in Oil section

new South Sudan and prosperous democracy. We will not have to be beholden to other countries we can use our own resources to rebuild our infrastructure, hospitals, schools, financial system, judiciary, military and police.

South Sudan will be just the first step. The marginalized areas of Sudan including Darfur and Nubian Mountains will finally get their promised vote on whether to join South Sudan. From there we will begin bringing true individual freedoms to all of Africa.

The East African trip was a turning point not only for Bol but the entire campaign. The trip raised awareness of how desperate the persecuted South Sudanese people are to get rid of the oppressive Kiir regime and how energized they are to fight for freedom. Bol's profile was definitely growing stronger on the world stage as shown by a large spread in the Sunday, July 8, 2018 *Washington Post*.[60]

Response to the *Post* article was immediate. Bol was invited to address the annual meeting of the Baptist General Convention of Virginia, an organization of eleven hundred African American churches in the state, the biggest group of its kind in the country. Bol shared the truth of what is happening in Africa today and his vision of what could be achieved there. He received a standing ovation. He has received invitations to speak to local churches and through those, donations to the campaign. Many more are needed.

The KDMP believes that the people's opportunity to participate in free, fair elections can only come after those who lust after power are not in charge of who holds it. But that is obviously not to be. The world community apparently has ceded the future of South Sudan to the very much feared Islamic Sudanese President Bashir, Uganda's President Museveni, South Sudanese President Kiir and his rival and former Vice President Machar. The four's "peace talks" in Khartoum led to a peace agreement formally signed in September

2018. All four of these leaders have blood on their hands. Sudan's Bashir is wanted by the International Criminal Court for genocide against the Sudanese and South Sudanese people. Who is he to decide leadership and peace terms for South Sudan?

Uganda's Museveni is in league with Kiir. Bol saw it first-hand in May when South Sudan's Director of Federal Security Gen Akol Koor had his agents (who carried Ugandan passports!) following us from the airport in Addis Ababa to and during our entire stay in Uganda. We believe we were somewhat protected by our American citizenship but that did not stop Koor's harassment nor Uganda's part in allowing South Sudanese agents free rein against us in Uganda. Local police were also forced to shut down some of our activities. Others have also documented Uganda's unsavory collaboration with Kiir.

Sudan's Bashir regime has openly declared it wants South Sudan back and only Muslims have the right to live there. This 2018 peace agreement took place in Khartoum where Bol and thousands of other South Sudanese were enslaved by the very man who is witnessing the signing? It is unacceptable and violates the sovereignty of South Sudan. The transitional constitution of 2011 derives its authority from "the will of the people" and "sovereignty is vested in the people." Where are the people in this unconstitutional "peace process'?

To its credit, the United States announced its refusal to go along with the "Evil Four's" so-called peace agreement. US Ambassador Nikki Haley on July 13, 2018 won the backing of the United Nations Security Council to impose for the first time a globally enforceable arms embargo on weapons sales and transfers to South Sudan.

The Kush Democratic Majority Party is pushing ahead. Its next stop is Juba, South Sudan where Presidential nominee Bol Gai Deng with thousands of people who want their freedom will stand on Freedom Square and demand the demand that Kiir and his regime step down immediately. If the East African trip had scary moments about security, it is nothing to what Bol, party leaders and supporters will be up against as they face the proverbial lions, President Kiir and his security director General Koor, in their very protected den.

Chapter 12

SUMMER 2018: ON THE GROUND IN SOUTH SUDAN

Conditions in South Sudan have become so hopeless that some of the younger citizens are beginning to speak out against the Kiir regime, despite knowing that doing so will probably cost them their lives. They understand all too well what they face, indeed some have already paid a high price.

Juba media reports that in July 2018 thirty teenagers were rounded up and detained at Juba International Airport by General Koor's National Security forces.

Most of the young men work as 'hawkers." They earn money by selling water, cigarettes, food, and other convenience items at the airport. The victims said security men stuffed them into a metal shipping container for several hours and then they were taken to a small National Security detention camp in nearby Luri where for nearly two weeks they were tortured.

One victim, Dudu Athian told journalist Ayuel Chan that he is a student at the Juba Institute of Nursing and was waiting to board a bus to take him to class around 9am on Friday, July 6th. Chan, a professional journalist, works for the SSBC, a government media house in Juba. He has been posting updates on his Facebook page.[61]

"Athian said a NS (National Security) vehicle pulled over and asked him to get in since he 'fits the description of people they were looking for,'" Chan reported. Unfortunately, Athian did not have identification with him at the time but did show them his papers from the school.

Athian said the boys were "subjected to sleep while standing for days due to limited space, tortured every day as well as forced to labor in a farm" on one small meal a day.

Despite National Security assurances that the boys would soon be released, it wasn't until eleven days later that 17 were let go. Sixteen are still unaccounted for.

"Due to fears of reprisal," the journalist said, "Athian was the only victim willing to share his story." He told Chan that "he now fears for his life and is very traumatized about starting over."

Among the other victims who refused to speak out is Garang Dut. Chan reports that Dut had a mental breakdown a few days after being released. He quotes sources as saying that Garang "spent four days walking completely naked in the streets of Juba before his relatives, who had spent days searching, eventually found him.

Garang, violent at the beginning and unwilling to talk to his relatives, was chased down, tied up and taken to hospital" where his wounds were being treated.

Aweil community elders are outraged at the arrests.

They have held a series of crisis meetings and have scheduled a meeting with President Kiir.

The Security Service said the boys were detained because they were in the process of leaving Juba to join General Paul Malong's revolt against President Kiir. The victims' families and friends adamantly deny that. They said the boys were being racially profiled, targeted because they were from Aweil.

Aweil is the hometown of General Malong, who was ousted earlier in 2018 as Kiir's Army of Chief of Staff. Malong was fired and placed under house arrest amid fears he was plotting against the regime. Later, his successor, James Ajonga Mawut, was poisoned. Regime critics said Mawut's death came on orders of the Security Director Koor.

Other young South Sudanese have died at the hands of what residents describe as "phantom" gunmen. In January, three sons of the Kuac family, Dr. Deng Muor Kuac and his brothers, attorney Ayuel Muor Kuac and Kon Muor Kuac were killed, witnesses said, by 15 members of government security forces. They said the team converged on the Kuac home in the Jebel Dinka residential area of Juba and killed the brothers in front of their mother. Neighbors afterward took their grief-stricken mother to the hospital and she died later that night.

KDMP's Chairman and candidate for President, Bol believes the current targeting of educated South Sudanese is an effort to wipe out any possible opponents to the regime among the younger generations. Some of the victims are people who have used social media to promote Bol's campaign. Bol says the regime has a list of 40 KDMP supporters in South Sudan who are to be eliminated. As earlier noted, the danger had made many reluctant to participate in social media activity on Bol's behalf.

Bol and the KDMP are well-known in South Sudan and across the world. The Sudanese are a closely-knit people both from their culture and to protect themselves from the oppression and violence they have endured for centuries.

Bol's cell phone is constantly ringing 24 hours a day. Anxious callers weigh in from Juba, Aweil, Nubia Mountains, Ruweng, and the refugee camps. He hears from widows of murdered South Sudanese generals, former leaders in the pre-independent SPLM/SPLA movement, frequent pleas from students and young leaders who are threatened with arrest and seeing increasing persecution for daring to speak out.

As previously indicated, the measure of KDMP's impact is seen by the attention paid to Bol and his supporters from the Kiir regime. Security Services Director Koor's appearance at Bol's East African rallies, threatening Bol's security team and shutting down their events, government names appearing on Facebook watching his live online interviews and speeches, even Kiir's earlier efforts to take over South Sudanese groups in the USA give testament to the regime's concern.

However, a growing number of young people now realize their only hope for change is to speak out against the Kiir administration's persecution of all ethnic groups, including Kiir's own Dinka. They are directly contacting Bol's Kush Democratic Majority Party (KDMP) which they believe is the only hope of bringing peace and prosperity to South Sudan. They say KDMP needs to act quickly in the face of efforts to extend Kiir's tenure.

Their hope is now hanging by a thread. Kiir and his allies are seeing success on a number of fronts that does not portend well for the future of South Sudan. On September 12, 2018. President Kiir and his former Vice President Riek Machar signed the new peace deal brokered by Sudan's Bashir and Uganda's Museveni. Bol says all four of these leaders have blood on their hands and "it is beyond cruel to force us to succumb to our tormentors—I still carry the scars from the chains with which Bashir's minions enslaved me at age seven."

Bol is just one among millions who have suffered persecution. A 2018 United Nations report charges that in a five-week period between April and May at least 232 people were killed and 112 girls and women were sexually assaulted by South Sudanese forces and allies in 40 opposition-held villages. The UN investigation found that elderly and disabled citizens were burned alive, others were hung from trees or had their throats slit. Some were shot as they fled.

The investigators reported girls and women were raped or gang-raped, and the victims included one who had recently given birth and "was still bleeding from labor." Those who resisted were shot. A 14-year-old girl told investigators, "How can I forget the sight of an old man whose throat was slit with a knife before being set on fire?"

"How can I forget the smell of those decomposed bodies of old men and children pecked and eaten by birds? Those women that were hanged and died up in the tree?"

Bol charges that "Bashir and Museveni, with the corrupt South Sudanese leaders Kiir and Machar, have brokered a selfish deal dividing power and resources for themselves, not to help the desperate people of South Sudan." The deal would extend Kiir's term 36 months under a provisional government that includes former Vice President Machar.

"Sudan's Bashir is wanted by the International Criminal Court for genocide and other crimes against humanity," Bol reminds the world community. He points to July 29, 2018 news reports that a Sudanese female journalist had been arrested and may face death for alleged crimes against the state. Women's rights activist and journalist Wini Omar appeared in court facing charges of prostitution and violating public morals, the Guardian newspaper reported. She was told she could also face further charges of spying against the Sudanese government. Omar's supporters said she is being targeted by Bashir's government because of her human rights work in the country.

"This is the very dictator who continues to perpetrate the persecution and genocide on Christians in the South and the marginalized people of the North," Bol argues, "Who is Bashir to decide leadership and peace terms for South Sudan?"

Independent observers say that Uganda's Museveni had been secretly siding with Kiir against Machar throughout previous unsuccessful peace talks led by the Intergovernmental Authority on Development (IGAD), an eight–country trade block in Africa. Each signed peace agreement failed, some after only a few hours.

Bol reminds that he experienced the Museveni government's bias first hand during his May trip to East Africa. South Sudan's Security forces tried to intimidate supporters at KDSP events in Uganda and successfully demanded that the local police chief shut down KDMP's activities. Bol notes that the current peace deal was signed in Khartoum, Sudan where he and fellow South Sudanese were enslaved by the very man who brokered the peace deal.

There are many other skeptics of this new peace agreement, including the US, Britain and Norway, but this Troika, other than pushing for "significant changes" in exchange for its support, is apparently standing on the sidelines. There has been repeated violence during and since the August 2018 Khartoum Declaration that included a ceasefire. Thirteen aid workers have been killed, civilian attacks have continued and monitoring teams have been denied timely access.

The Troika's demand for changes includes: an end to the violence, full humanitarian access, government accountability and transparency in the use of resources for the benefit of all South Sudanese. These are the same demands that have been enumerated through countless peace agreements. None has been honored. "The situation is tragic and deteriorating," says Bol, "and it also poses a long-term danger to the West, especially my adopted United States."

Bol argues that the US must not give place to warlords who are only concerned about power. "America should stand with the South

Sudanese people who have voiced their wishes through the Kush Democratic Majority Party." Ninety percent of the people want Kiir gone.

"Kiir continues to use the shadowy playbook that he and the late Dr. Garang followed from the beginning of the second rebellion in 1983. South Sudan's Parliament in the summer of 2018 voted to extend Kiir's term until 2021 after which the 400 lawmakers were given 'loans' of $40,000 each, an amount that would take an average South Sudanese worker several years to earn. The bonuses have been widely criticized by opposition politicians and human rights organizations.

Kiir is also agreeing to use increasing oil revenues to pay its remaining $1.2-billion-dollar oil debt to financially-strapped Sudan. Bashir, facing widespread food and fuel shortages, dissolved Sudan's government September 9, 2018 and appointed a new prime minister."

Bol and others charge that China is exploiting Sudan's economic crisis for political and economic advantages. September 2018 news reports reveal Bashir's promise of concessions and protection of Chinese companies in Sudan, Bashir's second visit to Beijing, and China's planned 60 billion dollar investment in Africa. An estimated one million Chinese have moved to Africa in the last ten years.

Temple University's Dr. Molefi Asante is clearly disturbed after returning from his September 2018 trip to Africa. The noted African American scholar found that the Chinese are making their presence felt all over South Sudan. "They are taking over Juba," he told Bol Gai Deng after visiting that nation's capital. Molefi also says the late Libyan leader Colonel Muammar Gaddafi trained the northern Nigerian tribe Funoni to do to Christians in South Nigeria what the Arab Islamic militants are doing in South Sudan. The same methods are also being employed in Mali, Central African Republic, Jibouti,

Mauritania, Chad and others. "The Muslims are taking over all of Africa—and with Communist China as a partner—they are expediting the elimination of Africans and their culture."

As the crackdown on dissidents and everyday citizens grows harsher and more widespread, young South Sudan's fragile independence becomes increasingly at risk.

Bol fears the country could break completely apart at any time and says that "would make largely Christian South Sudan vulnerable to takeover by Islamic Sudan with the aid of China and Russia who both have forces on the ground" in South Sudan. "My grandfather was among the leaders who held off Sharia law for more than a hundred years," says Bol, "South Sudan needs America's help to prevent it now.

"The KDMP cannot stand by and let corrupt leaders continue to trade South Sudan for power," Bol says. "We must go to Juba and demand that Kiir step down. It is the only avenue left to my people who are facing death and imprisonment if they act before we arrive.

"I am an American citizen, a Christian South Sudanese citizen and former slave who has dealt with these terrorists all my life. I have personally suffered at their hands. They are afraid of America's power and will bend to her demands if she has the fortitude to make them." Bol strongly believes that "this is the time for America to take charge and provide protection for one of her own. As I go to face down Kiir, Machar and Bashir, I don't go to become a ruler," Bol asserts. "I go to demand that the people decide by the ballot box who they want to lead them.

"In East Africa I met with thousands of our people from every tribe--a younger generation of college-educated and proven leaders who are determined that our country will fulfill the promise of our independence of 2011. During my trip I talked with Kush Democratic Majority Party leaders from the refugee camps in Ethiopia, Uganda and Kenya as well as South Sudan, South Sudanese student group leaders from universities across the region, and heads of churches both from South Sudan and the marginalized areas of Sudan. We also met with countless refugees who came, on their own, to tell me of their struggles and desire to return home to live in peace and resume their lives."

Bol sums up the situation this way: "what is going on in Africa is evil and the eradication of that evil must start in South Sudan. My people have the courage to do what is necessary--and the world community has the obligation to press for Kiir's resignation and provide ballot security for voters in the country and her refugees by absentee ballot around the world.

Ruthless dictators bent on looting South Sudan's resources must be stopped," he says, "and the United States, who raised our hopes for an independent South Sudan, has a special interest in ensuring that those hopes are not destroyed forever. America must get engaged in Africa."

Epilogue

OUR VISION OF SOUTH SUDAN'S FUTURE

The air smells of raw, fresh lumber and the sounds of hammers pounding nails and bricks being tapped into place, a cacophony of industriousness as walls for home after home are raised. At first the return is a trickle. A few people cautiously appearing, loaded down with bundles of ragged belongings and holding tightly to their small children, eyes darting about alert for danger. As word spread, larger groups started coming and then flooding in as millions of formerly displaced South Sudanese began to believe that true peace was here at last. A budding hope replacing despair. What was left of several generations of families together began the hot, dusty trek, returning home after years of living in squalid refugee camps or hiding in the bush.

There is a slowly growing sense throughout Juba and stretching to smaller towns and villages that finally their nightmare is over. No more sinister shadows of phantoms carrying guns, stealing into homes and spiriting away the vulnerable to sell into slavery while leaving the bodies of fathers and sons in their wake. So many terror-filled years had left a deep uncertainty that life could ever be normal, but just the sheer need for food, sleep and daily living forces residents to set aside their fears and just get on with it. Everyone needs a place to live and workers are needed to build homes, apartments and buildings to house businesses that will feed the growing demand for the necessities of a dignified life without war.

The landscape changes. Fields plowed and planted, roads, bridges and train tracks completed making travel virtually effortless, pealing church bells calling the faithful. Neighborhoods no longer pierced by screams of anguish.

The atmosphere slowly softens: mommies singing soft lullabies to their babies, men whistling as they worked, the laughter of children deep into a no-holds-barred football game. South Sudan begins to shift. Self-respect and pride of home are beginning to take hold as women, no longer forced to hide away from attackers, can shop, visit and use their talents to build small businesses. Schools are filled with their children by day and adults learning computer and high tech skills at night.

It had been so hard to believe that better times were coming. Hard to persuade hearts that there were people willing to set aside their own carefree life across the sea and come home to lead their native country. To risk their own lives and stand up to brutal, corrupt regimes and say, "NO MORE."

Kiir Akol, Aweil Community Chairman in Kenya long ago made up his mind and challenges his generation:

"The future belongs to us, youths who must reject blood money given to them to hunt down their own brothers and sisters in order to please a master who cannot take our country into the digital world. A master who would rather park millions of dollars under his bed because he has no idea of what to do with money.

Pick a leader who will keep jobs in your country by offering companies incentives to hire only within their borders, not one who allows corporations to outsource jobs for cheaper labor when there is a national employment crisis. Choose a leader who will invest in building bridges, not walls. Books, not weapons. Morality, not corruption. Intellectualism and wisdom, not ignorance. Stability, not fear and terror.

Peace, not tribalism. From national level to state level. Love, not hate. Convergence, not segregation. Tolerance, not discrimination.

Fairness, not hypocrisy. Substance, not superficiality. Character, not immaturity. Transparency, not secrecy. Justice, not lawlessness. Environmental improvement and preservation, not destruction. Truth, not lies.

South Sudan belongs to all South Sudanese. Do not threaten people, there will be a time when you will need them."

That time is now. Choose your future not based on fear but faith, character, courage and destiny. Join the unified Kush Democratic Majority Party and together we will change history.

ACKNOWLEDGMENTS

I proudly come from the people of Mading Aweil, Wun-Booth Anyaar, Malual Gier Nyang, Malaul Tueng, and the Muoyjang or Jieng of Dinka Malual of South Sudan and Sudan. Nothing I have done would have been possible without my childhood spent the midst of this great African culture. Mading Aweil's strong grounding in discipline and the peace-making people in Muoyjang or Jieng Society of Sudan have my deepest thanks.

The 22 kingdoms in Aweil Region continue working tirelessly to maintain the peace among Aweil people and across South Sudan and Sudan. They should never be taken for granted. I would not be here if they had not taught my people democratic rights as the fundamental African and Mouyjang or Jieng core values. We believe in fairness, justice, and equality for everyone: poor, rich, blind, disabled, child, female and male. South Sudan's government should treat all with the same human dignity and respect.

Human dignity is the motto of Mading, Aweil Chiefdoms. These kings are the champion of African Democracy and the Muoyjang people of the Nile valley, Neolithic, who are the only people in Africa Continent who have never been ruled by any external kings or queens. Our Spiritual Team, or Community of Faith was created September 22, 2012 in a 14 mile area known as Kiirkou, Kiir Adem, and Warguet in Aweil State. This area that had never been included during (CPA) comprehensive peace agreement as part of North Sudan is acknowledged. Here are their names: Late Anyeng Anei Yor. Abuk Buk Piol. Abuna (Rev) Mou Mou. Rev. Aken Tong Yel. Angeer Arou Lual. Ernest Kuei Madut Akuei. Abuk Baak. Abuk Dhieu Achien. Achan Achor Thiel. Ayak Akuei Akuei. Wol Wol Wol Dut. Achai Kawach Makuei. Ker Aleu Deng. Ajak Anet. Athieng Amaal. Akecdit Dut Baak. Abuk chier Deng. Dut Marieu Mawien Tong.

The Aweil Youth Union leaders liberated many of us from Arab slave traders and the Sudan slave auction in the Southern Kordofan Region in 1985. The Aweil Youth Union under the leadership of Ustaze Kiir Majok Kiir, rescued our families in 1988 from war, slavery and starvation. These heroes names are Kiir Majok Kiir, Kuel Aguer Kuel. Aweil 's former governor. Gabriel Kuot Kuot Rev. Rev. Aken Tong Yel. Angelo Atak Akol. Lual Lual Agau, Chandit Geng Ariath. John Atak. Garang Garang, Angelo Atak Akol, Chandit Geng Araith, and Ungec Yangkor Ungec, There are many others. in South Sudan and Sudan. Late Anyeng Anei Yor. Abuk

Buk Piol, Angeer Arou Lual, Abuk Baak. Abuk Dhieu Achien. Achan Achor Thiel. Ayak Akuei Akuei, Achai Kawach Makuei, Ajak Anet. Athieng Amaal. Akecdit Dut Baak, and Abuk chier Deng.

Sudanese brothers and sisters in the fight for justice: historian Tanutamon Gerais; he was once a Muslim named Khalid but changed to a great African name of Tanutamon after discovering his true African identity, Niemat Ahmadi, Director of Darfur Woman Action group, the greatest human right activist women in Sudan and the African Continent as whole and, the great Sudanese human rights activist Dr. Abdelgabar Adam.

I want to acknowledge those who put the Pan Africanism and the New Sudan vision as the blue print to liberate every African woman and man in old Sudan, the Marginalized people of Sudan.

Finally, I want to pay tribute to the memory of the late Brian Staples who died serving the people of South Sudan and Sudan. Brian Staples was the first white student from Virginia Commonwealth University to reach my tiny village in 2012.

NOTES

1. http://www.saudiembassy.net/about/country-information/facts_and_figures/

2. Nasr, Seyyed (2005). Mecca, The Blessed, Medina, The Radiant: The Holiest Cities of Islam.

3. The Nuer Religion, Professor E. E. Evans-Pritchard, 1956. https://archive.org/stream/nuerrProfessor

4. New World Encyclopedia, Jennifer Tanabe, November 16, 2015. http://www.newworldencyclopedia.org/p/index.php?title=Kingdom_of_Kush&oldid=992041,

5. Egypt Before the Pharaohs, Antoine Gigal, 2013-2015. http://gigalresearch.com/uk/publications-pharaohs.php

6. "The Egyptian Sudan," J. Kelley Giffen, 1902. https://archive.org/details/in.ernet.dli.2015.502212

7. Ancient Kingdoms in Land of War, Isma'il Kush Kush, New York Times, March 31, 2013.

8. One World Nations online, Publisher and Editor in Chief Klaus Kästle, 2015. http://www.nationsonline.org/oneworld/historical_countryn ames.htm

9. The Rich History of the Ancient Nubian Kingdom of Dongola, DHWTY, July 9, 2015. http://www.ancient-origins.net/ancient-places-africa/rich-history-ancient-nubian-kingdom-dongola-003387

10. https://en.wikipedia.org/wiki/%27Amr_ibn_al-%27As

11. http://www.africanews.com/2018/03/15/south-su-dan-seeks-to-join-arab-league-the-morning-call/"/south-sudan-seeks-to-join-arab-league-the-morning-call/

12. https://www.facebook.com/suzan.aguer/videos/1718650521576103/?fref=mentions

13. The Egyptian Sudan, Giffen, 1902.

14. Renaming of Schools on Back Burner, Justin Mattingly, Richmond Times Dispatch, September 10, 2018.

15. Oil Company Defends Role in Sudan, Bernard Simon, New York Times, October 17, 2001.3

16. http://www.theeastafrican.co.ke/news/Iran--Sudan-liable-for-1998-embassy-bombings/2558-1291064-pqql7h/index.html"h/index.html

17. Oil Company Defends Role in Sudan, Bernard Simon, New York Times, October 17, 2001

18. https://www.theguardian.com/world/2001/oct/17/afghanista n.terrorism3

19. https://www.independent.co.uk/news/world/anti-soviet-warrior-puts-his-army-on-the-road-to-peace-the-saudi-businessman-who-recruited-mujahedin-1465715.html

20. https://www.theguardian.com/world/2001/oct/17/afghanista n.terrorism3

21. https://www.npr.org/2011/05/02/135905649/
bin-laden-from-millionaires-son-to-most-wanted"/
bin-laden-from-millionaires-son-to-most-wanted

22. https://morningstarnews.org/2017/05/pastor-chris-
tian-activist-sentenced-prison-sudan-released/"/
pastor-christian-activist-sentenced-prison-sudan-released/

23. Mark 16:15 New Testament, Holy Bible.

24. Mahdist Revolution (1881-1898), www.blackpast.org

25. Human Rights Abuses in Sudan in 1987, Ushari Ahmed
Mahmud and Suleyman Ali Baldo, September 1987.

26. https://www.nationalgeographic.com/archae-
ology-and-history/magazine/2016/11-12/
ancient-egypt-nubian-kingdom-pyramids-sudan/"/
ancient-egypt-nubian-kingdom-pyramids-sudan/

27. The Rescue of Jerusalem, the Alliance between Hebrews and
Africans in 701 BC, by Henry T. Aubin, 2002.

28. http://www.catholic.org/saints/saint.php?saint_id=5601

29. "The Arab Project" was a term coined by Temple University
professor Dr. Molefi Kete Asante during "The Marginalized
People of Sudan" conference at Temple University, Philadelphia, Pennsylvania, 2012.

30. http://www.salem-news.com/articles/july152010/al-bashir-
south-wd.php

31. https://pulitzercenter.org/reporting/ south-sudan-failed-state-lobby

32. https://www.hurstpublishers.com/ terror-and-crisis-in-sudans-blue-nile/

33. https://www.newsweek.com/slave-auctions-libya-smug-glers-are-selling-migrants-400-dollars-710623

34. https://wakeupethiopians.wordpress.com/2013/03/01/ arabs-hate-black-people-they-dont-think-a-black-can-be-muslim/

35. Temple University Professor Dr. Molefi Kete Asante, "The Marginalized People of Sudan conference, Temple University, Philadelphia, Pennsylvania, 2012.

36. Washington Post, South Sudan's Government-Made Famine, Global Opinions by George Clooney and John Prendergast, March 9, 2017.

37. https://www.reuters.com/article/ us-southsudan-security-un-exclusive/exclusive-south-su-dans-government-using-food-as-weapon-of-war-u-n-report-idUSKBN1DA2OX"OX

38. https://www.hrw.org/world-report/2018/country-chapters/ south-sudan"/country-chapters/south-sudan

39. http://www.christianitytoday.com/edstetzer/2017/novem-ber/ south-sudan-famine-war-and-hope.html

40. https://www.unicefusa.org/mission/emergencies/conflict/ so uth-sudan

41. https://www.thestar.com.my/news/environment/

42. https://www.dw.com

43. http://via.news/africa/briefing-big-oil-contamination-south-sudan/

44. https://www.reuters.com/article/us-southsudan-oil/south-sudan-aims-to-more-than-double-oil-output-in-2017-18-idUSKBN15B1CD

45. Fueling Atrocities: Oil and War in South Sudan, https://the-sentry.org/

46. https://theconversation.com/oil-fuels-the-conflict-between-sudan-and-south-sudan-and-it-keeps-getting-hotter

47. China's Foreign Policy Experiment in South Sudan, July 10, 2017, https://www.crisisgroup.org/africa/horn-africa/south-sudan/

48. Oil Production in South Sudan: Making it a Benefit for All, Baseline Assessment of the Impact of Oil Production on Communities in Upper Nile and Unity States, Summary Report May 2014. https://www.cordaid.org/

49. Dinka scholars argue that the name derives from the Dinka words "Khier-tuom" which translates to a "place where rivers meet". This is supported by historical accounts which place the Dinka homeland in central Sudan as late as the 13th-15th centuries A.D."Place names of the World", Adrian Room, 2006.

50. https://joelstrumpet.com/ethiopia-and-sudan-in-biblical-prophecy/North

51. Proverbs 29:18 Old Testament, Holy Bible, KJV.

52. Arab Racism in Kush, The Adventures and Opinions of Bol Gai Deng, Universal Write Publications, 2016

53. https://www.theguardian.com/world/2001/oct/17/afghanista n.terrorism

54. http://www.salem-news.com/articles/july152010/al-bashir-south-wd.php

55. American Epiphany (AE) is a US-registered 501 (c)(3) non profit organization dedicated to supporting creative projects to promote awareness and appreciation of the US Declaration of Independence and US Constitution. AE has been a long-time supporter of Bol Gai Deng's efforts to tell stories to promote awareness and bring freedom, peace and prosperity to South Sudan and the marginalized people of Sudan.

56. Nazar Suliman is from the Nuba Mountains, Sudan. His humanitarian work and protests against the government led him to serving 18 months in an Egyptian prison before the US intervened. Nazar became an American citizen in 2010.

57. The Everyday Guide to the Bible, by Carol Smith, 2002 by Barbour Publishing Company.

58. Kush Democratic Majority Party organizational meeting, Juba, South Sudan, 2014.

59. Excerpts from April 7, 2017 speech by Bol Gai Deng announcing his candidacy for President of South Sudan from the Kush Democratic Majority Party. www.kushdemocraticmajority.org.

60. https://www.washingtonpost.com/local/virginia-politics/
by-day-he-runs-for-president-of-south-sudan-by-night-he-
unloads-trucks-at-lowes/

61. https://www.facebook.com/AyuelChan. July 30, 2018.

Appendix

RULES AND REGULATIONS OF THE KUSH DEMOCRATIC MAJORITY PARTY

The name shall be the Kush Democratic Majority Party.

Definitions:

Chairman is the head of a committee and may be either a man or a woman.

District Committee shall mean the committee of a particular region or section of the South Sudanese People.

Dates: This refers to dates for holding elections. If the date should fall on a day holiday or religious day then the election will be held on the next day.

Elector is one who is duly registered into he KDM and is in good standing to vote on candidates for the KDM.

Membership means all of those people who are enrolled as members of the KDM.

Quorum is one third of the membership in a particular region. Business can be conducted if one third of the members are present.

District is a sub-division of the South Sudan nation.

RULE 1 VOTER QUALIFICATIONS FOR HOLDING MEMBERSHIP IN KDM

ARTICLE 1: Any qualified elector is allowed to vote in elections.

ARTICLE 2: Any elector shall be allowed to run for office as a delegate, committee members, or officers.

ARTICLE 3. All members of committees must be qualified members of the Kush Democratic Majority in good standing.

ARTICLE 4. No person shall hold office as chairman of a committee unless the majority of the committee has voted for him or her.

RULE 2 ORGANIZATION OF THE PARTY

ARTICLE 1 The organization of the party shall consist of six districts.

ARTICLE 2 Membership in the district committees.

ARTICLE 3 All members of the district committees shall be in good standing in their districts.

RULE 3 ELECTIONS

The Kush Democratic Majority shall govern the terms of elections. Each election shall be opened to all people included as members.

RULE 4 MEETINGS

Meetings shall be held every third Monday.

KUSH
DEMOCRATIC
MAJORITY
PARTY